RACING
TOGETHER
1949 - 2016

EDITED BY NICK HARRIS
FOREWORDS BY VITO IPPOLITO, CARMELO EZPELETA AND HERVÉ PONCHARAL

Published in November 2017

ISBN 978-1-910505-24-3

Published by Evro Publishing
Westrow House, Holwell, Sherborne,
Dorset DT9 5LF, UK

Printed and bound in Slovenia by GPS Group

Editorial Director: Mark Hughes
Designer: Richard Parsons

This book is produced in association with Dorna Sports SL, owners of the MotoGP™, Moto2™ and Moto3™ trademarks (© Dorna Sports SL 2017)

www.evropublishing.com

CONTENTS

FOREWORDS

PART 1
THE DORNA STORY

The nine MotoGP race winners of 2016 (from left): Jorge Lorenzo, Valentino Rossi, Jack Miller, Marc Márquez, Andrea Iannone, Cal Crutchlow, Maverick Viñales, Dani Pedrosa and Andrea Dovizioso.

FOREWORD
VITO IPPOLITO
PRESIDENT, FÉDÉRATION INTERNATIONALE
DE MOTOCYCLISME (FIM)

In a world that is changing so much and moving so fast, celebrating 25 years of cooperation as we are doing today is something of tremendous value. Four different organizations, with fundamentally differing roles, have worked together to create the uncontested success of MotoGP. We do indeed feel very proud of this achievement. FIM, Dorna, MSMA and IRTA have demonstrated a great capacity to understand one another and work with intelligence and passion to make our sport great.

During these 25 years, there have been some difficult moments and we can say with satisfaction that we have not only overcome them successfully but that in doing so we have exceeded all expectations. I am thinking for instance of the passage from two-stroke to four-stroke engines in all classes, the global financial crisis of 2008, and the need to find appropriate technical solutions to enhance the spectacular aspect of the sport. It is also worth highlighting the convergence of our efforts to improve the safety of our riders. This priority has been constantly present in all the decisions taken and we have achieved impressive results.

Our sport represents one of the great syntheses of the modern world: the balance between human being and machine. To achieve this, in other words, to place a human individual and a motorcycle on a track to demonstrate the progress of technology and at the same time the extraordinary skills of the riders, some of which are the stuff of legend, has been a challenge for all of us. And in every race and every season, we have been able to appreciate the results. Moreover, in 2016, the year of the 25th anniversary, we have been treated to an exceptionally high level of performance.

This celebration is not only a reflection of 25 years of working together. It is also fully justified by the success we have obtained and which, to crown it all, has been corroborated by the public: the huge numbers of spectators who flock to the circuits in all corners of the world and follow us on all types of media. The figures achieved defy our imagination. This is the reward for the combined efforts of the FIM, Dorna, MSMA and IRTA and all those who have worked with us to make it possible.

I am sure that, a few years further down this road that we have traced together, we shall all have the pleasure of celebrating once more.

The past 25 years have been a dream for the Championship, including the relationship between the four main bodies: the FIM, Dorna, the MSMA and IRTA. Unfortunately, I am old enough to remember how it was before — and everything was a lot more difficult!

VITO IPPOLITO

FOREWORD
CARMELO EZPELETA PEIDRO
CHIEF EXECUTIVE OFFICER, DORNA

It makes us very proud to be able to celebrate the 25th anniversary of the collaboration between the FIM, Dorna, the MSMA and IRTA, and celebrate a quarter of a century together in motorcycle racing. Since our collaboration began, a lot of new chapters in the history of MotoGP have been written, and it is an honour for us to look forward to writing so many more.

The 2016 MotoGP season was the 25th anniversary year and it was one where we celebrated in style. A record-breaking and historic season with nine different winners in the premier class — the first time that had happened — made it a true benchmark in the 68-year history of the sport and a fitting year for us to celebrate this milestone. We also celebrated the 400th GP of this new era in Brno, which was a race that gave us one of the incredible eight different winners in a row and another historic moment.

After the year of landmarks and records, the bar was set high for 2017. But this golden era has continued and the racing and records are more incredible than ever. It makes us proud to see the foundations we have laid for 25 years consistently producing some of the greatest racing in the world.

Those foundations we have laid together are strong, and we continue to build more. With the Road to MotoGP, our talent-promotion programmes and our persistent investment in the present and potential of our sport, we can look forward to a bright future.

Since the time the lights first went out in the Motorcycle Grand Prix World Championship in 1949, we have seen heroes emerge, legends crafted, and some of the most extraordinary stories in racing — stories that we keep adding to today. A lot of things have changed since both the beginning of the World Championship and the beginning of our collaboration, but one thing has always and will continue to stay the same: the passion for the sport; in all of us, in the paddock and the competitors, and in the grandstands. That is what makes sharing so much of this journey in the history of the sport so special.

I hope, in 25 years, we can celebrate another quarter of a century of this collaboration and look forward to another 25.

CARMELO EZPELETA PEIDRO

FOREWORD
HERVÉ PONCHARAL
PRESIDENT, INTERNATIONAL ROAD RACING TEAMS ASSOCIATION (IRTA)

The priority and the role of IRTA was always to take care of the safety of the riders first, and in that we have always had incredible support from Dorna. I would like to thank Carmelo Ezpeleta, Dorna CEO, for that. I remember many years ago when Daijiro Kato had his accident, a very difficult moment for all of us, Carmelo said we would not go back to Suzuka unless the circuit was changed. And everyone said that one day we would return there, but we never went back. That is just one example of what we have achieved together: making circuits safer, no longer visiting dangerous circuits and always improving the level of safety — something incredibly important for everyone in the Championship.

The second job of IRTA is to take care of the day-to-day lives of the teams, which includes having more financial support from the Championship, and that is what we are doing every year. I think the past 25 years have seen the lives of each team — in Moto3, Moto2 and MotoGP — getting better and better, and they are better and better supported by the Championship. Life is a lot easier now, and it will keep improving in this aspect as last year we once again renewed and strengthened our contract to continue building for the future.

In addition, in the MotoGP class, the evolution of the Championship in terms of the regulations has brought the Independent and Factory teams closer together. One tyre, one ECU, one aerodynamic evolution in the season, a limit on the number of engines… these things have also helped IRTA a lot. IRTA is the International Road Racing Teams Association, so we take care of the teams. And these past 25 years have seen life for the teams getting better and better, as I said, in all three classes. We are always consulted about everything and have an active role.

Now, all the main decisions are taken by the Grand Prix Commission, where you have one member of each board: one FIM, one Dorna, one MSMA and one IRTA. Most of the decisions taken are now unanimous, which is an incredible step forward from how it was before, when there was always a lot of discussion and disagreement — sometimes with radically different points of view. And now, as I said, decisions are so often unanimous.

I would like to thank Dorna and especially Dorna CEO Carmelo Ezpeleta for having built and created this incredible, positive atmosphere, and for making the Championship grow. Seeing the remarkable progress we have made over 25 years, we can be sure that the future will only continue this positive trend as we look ahead.

HERVÉ PONCHARAL

PART 1
THE DORNA STORY
THE 25-YEAR REVOLUTION

2017 FIM MotoGP™

All the hard work of the past 25 years has resulted in this incredible line-up of machinery at the start of the 2017 MotoGP season in Qatar.

LD CHAMPIONSHIP

CHAPTER 1
FOUNDATIONS
BY DENNIS NOYES

¿QUIÉN?... WHO?

On 26 October 1990, no one at the Fédération Internationale de Motocyclisme (FIM) General Assembly in Budapest, Hungary, had a cell phone. When newly elected FIM President Jos Vaessen announced the name of the winning company in the bidding for the GP television rights, several in the large audience stood and hurried up the aisle in search of one of the very few phones in the lobby.

Most people in that large auditorium expected the president to name one of the well-known, international sports marketing bidders: Bernie Ecclestone's ISC (International Sportsworld Communicators), Mark McCormack's IMG (International Management Group) or Maurizio Flammini's Flammini Racing. Instead he named a company almost no one in that assembly, representing world motorcycling, had ever heard of.

Just before I entered the auditorium that day, Dutchman Jaap Timmer in his wide-lapel, double-breasted suit, a former President of the powerful FIM Road Racing Commission and a leading member of ROPA (Road Race Organizers and Promoters Association), stopped me and asked, "Do you know of a company called Dorna?" I didn't, and he said, "You soon will."

As I think back on it now, I realize that there was an inkling in the air. In the short interval between the closed-door management council meeting and the beginning of the general assembly, word had gotten out that something completely surprising, something totally unforeseen, had happened. What Jaap Timmer told me had also reached many of the delegates from the 49 national federations and the eight associate members.

Instead of the usual hubbub before the call to order,

RIGHT Journalist Dennis Noyes (left) in position on the Spanish table at the history-making 1990 FIM General Assembly in Budapest. At the far end is the late Nicolás Rodil del Valle, FIM President from 1974 to 1989.

the congress floor was strangely hushed — like the charged quiet on the racing grid back in the days of push starts.

"I am proud to inform you," said Vaessen from the high rostrum after the brief opening formalities, "that the FIM has received a highest bid of 30 million dollars from the Spanish company, Dorna Promoción del Deporte."

There was a murmur from the floor: "War? *Wie? Chi? Qui? Quem? ¿Quién?* Who?"

A heated debate broke out on the floor of the assembly and the General Secretary of the Italian Federation proposed an immediate secret ballot with a yes or no vote on extending the bidding period to allow companies to increase their bids. He claimed that one of the companies had offered 32 million but Vaessen said that this was untrue. All bids received prior to the deadline had been sealed. Now, with a winner having been announced, he would not permit the assembly to vote on extending the period again. Instead, Vaessen called for a vote that would be "for the President and the Management Council continuing or not continuing negotiations with Dorna Promoción del Deporte." Tortured language, I thought; I had never covered this kind of story.

I was a motorcycle journalist, used to writing race reports, interviewing riders, but I was out of my element that day in Budapest. As President of IRRPA (International Road Racing Press Association) and because I wrote for a Spanish magazine, I was seated at the far end of the 'Spanish table' and in the prestigious company of Nicolás Rodil del Valle, FIM President from 1965 to 1983, Luis Soriano, former Spanish Federation President, Jorge Cabezas, FIM Vice President and, nearest to me, José Antonio Gil of the Spanish Federation and acting in representation of the Chilean Federation.

I didn't understand the significance, the nuance, of the change in the wording of what was being voted upon until someone seated near me — I think it was Jorge Cabezas — said in a stage whisper, "¡*Es un voto de confianza*!" He was right. It was, in essence if not literally, a vote of confidence.

Had the vote gone against him, Vaessen would have been expected to resign, but the vote was 66 to 17 (with four abstentions) in support of accepting the bid from Dorna.

The next day at the management council meeting, Francesco Zerbi, FIM Deputy President and second in command, offered his resignation because he had strongly opposed the President the day before during the TV rights debate. Vaessen didn't accept the resignation and expressed confidence in his Deputy President. The two shook hands and received the

applause of the council. Vaessen said he considered the matter closed.

But really it had only just begun. For the next two years the action on track between the likes of Wayne Rainey, Kevin Schwantz, Wayne Gardner, Eddie Lawson, Mick Doohan, John Kocinski and the other top 500cc, 250cc and 125cc riders would thrill television audiences, but behind the scenes the battle was for the control of the television itself and, finally, for the entire Grand Prix commercial and sporting package.

Years later I learned something surprising: the Management Council at Budapest, prior to the General Assembly, had already decided to reject the bid from Bernie Ecclestone's company. The council felt that Ecclestone's control of Formula One constituted a conflict of interests.

Mike Trimby, General Secretary of IRTA (International Road Racing Teams Association) and, in 1990, present in Budapest as delegate of the Hong Kong Federation, believes the decision by the FIM not even to entertain a bid from any Ecclestone company "was like a red cape to a bull. I think what most motivated Bernie after that was not so much losing in the bidding as having the FIM refuse to even consider his bid after it had been initially solicited and accepted by the FIM."

Background. In 1988 the FIM assigned a Swiss company, MotoMedia, formed by IRTA and ROPA and backed by the major tobacco sponsors of the championship, the authority to contract television rights to a specialist company. The company chosen was ISC, Bernie Ecclestone's ISC. The fee was $800,000 per year or half the gross ISC income, whichever was larger. The

ABOVE Dorna's model of the sturdy, unsinkable Galician fishing boat that provided the perfect company name.

and Promoters Association, and TWP is Two Wheel Promotions, a company formed by Ecclestone in 1991 for the purpose of managing motorcycle Grand Prix racing. The manufacturers later formed a group called the Grand Prix Manufacturers Association (GPMA) that later was renamed the Motorcycle Sport Manufacturers Association (MSMA).

Dorna, although sometimes incorrectly written in capital letters, is not an acronym. A *dorna* is a small, Galician vessel modelled on the ancient *drakkers* that carried Viking and Norman war parties on raids in the Middle Ages. Three of the four founders of Dorna were from Galicia and they named their aggressive, young sports marketing company after the sturdy little fishing boat with a reputation for being virtually unsinkable.

THE 'WORLD SERIES' THREAT

Even before the results of the bidding were announced, there had been rumours of a second attempt by Grand Prix team leaders to organize a 'World Series', inspired by the unsuccessful revolt led by Kenny Roberts and Barry Coleman against the FIM in 1979. Once again, Grand Prix motorcycle racing was at a crossroads between continued governance by the FIM and the very real possibility of the creation of a break-away, outlaw championship.

Bigger-than-life, swashbuckling characters from banking, big tobacco and sports marketing became entangled in a fierce struggle for FIM TV rights and, of all the persons who feature in this story, two principal players emerge: Englishman Bernie Ecclestone and Spaniard Carmelo Ezpeleta. Bernie started his motorsports career as a salesman of second-hand motorcycles and, briefly, as a fast but crash-prone motorcycle racer on both grass tracks and asphalt. Carmelo Ezpeleta abandoned university engineering studies to follow his passion for motorsports primarily as a rally driver and, on one occasion, co-driver in the Baja Aragon Rally with double World Champion Carlos Sainz. He also briefly raced motorcycles.

After the 1990 FIM Congress, IRTA formally joined forces with Ecclestone, leaving Dorna with TV rights to an FIM championship potentially without the top teams and riders. Ecclestone began to contact circuits and even managed to get his friend Max Mosley, President of the FIA (Fédération Internationale de l'Automobile), to begin discussions about modifying the association statutes to permit FIA sanctioning of motorcycle racing in direct competition with the FIM.

With growing uncertainty causing circuits and sponsors to doubt the level of the championship that the FIM and Dorna could field, Dorna opened talks with Ecclestone in 1991 and, in the end and after several reversals, all parties joined forces. The 1992 racing

ABOVE Bernie Ecclestone, seen here when he was pillion passenger with Randy Mamola at Estoril in 2001, was an early rival to Dorna for FIM rights. Later, as owner of TWP (Two Wheel Promotions), he briefly shared management of the MotoGP Championship before finally selling TWP to Dorna, exclusive promoter of the championship since 1993.

ISC contract covered the period from 1989 to 1992 and did not grant right of first refusal. In March 1990 the FIM Management Council decided not to renew the MotoMedia-ISC agreement. Instead, the council empowered President Vaessen to invite bidding on a five-year (1993–1997) contract.

Had Dorna executives known in 1990 what they would soon learn about the internal and external problems behind the scenes in the world of Grand Prix motorcycle racing, they might never have made that $30-million-dollar bid. Fortunately, however, they believed enough in the potential of the sport to outbid some of the most experienced motorsports management companies in the world. After Dorna won the bidding, Ecclestone and IRTA began working to create a parallel championship.

To identify the players and understand the background of the early Dorna years, familiarity with several acronyms and abbreviations is necessary, so let us recap on those already encountered and introduce a few more. FIM is the Fédération Internationale de Motocyclisme, IRTA is the International Road Racing Teams Association, ROPA is the Roadrace Organizers

season was run under an agreement between Dorna/FIM and TWP/IRTA. And then, toward the end of the '92 season, Dorna bought TWP and, finally, succeeded in acquiring not just the TV rights, but all commercial rights, including the contracting of circuits, the composition of the calendar and shared authority over sporting matters in conjunction with the FIM and IRTA.

I turned to Carmelo Ezpeleta to recount some of the key moments of those early years.

"In 1990," says Carmelo, "I was a member of ROPA in my capacity as representative of Jarama, and was well acquainted with ROPA ex-President Jaap Timmer and ROPA member Mauricio Flammini, who was the promoter of the Italian Grand Prix and would later promote the GPs in Yugoslavia and Czechoslovakia. I had helped Flammini find funding for his attempt to acquire the GP TV rights. After Dorna had outbid all the other companies, Flammini called to propose that we work together to try to buy the FIM rights from Dorna. He wondered, since Dorna had no motorsports experience, if they had merely bought for the purpose of selling the rights on.

"I knew of Dorna because of their activities in Spanish football and, through my neighbour Jesús Samper, who was Secretary General of the Spanish Professional Football League, I met with two of the Dorna principals. They assured me that Dorna, having recently sold 50 per cent of the company to Banesto, was fully committed to administering and marketing the TV rights. I recall they asked me, 'And why are you so interested in this?' I explained my involvement with the circuits and with ROPA, and the next question was, 'And how would you go about all this?'

"I told them that, in my opinion, they had a very serious problem because they had won the rights in competition with several companies and that among those companies was one owned by Bernie Ecclestone who had a very close relationship with IRTA. They didn't seem worried and told me that they were soon to have a meeting to present their plans to President Vaessen, and I said that they would be presenting to a group consisting of the FIM, IRTA and ROPA and that I would be there too."

That meeting did not go well and it became apparent to both the FIM and Dorna that Dorna lacked sufficient expertise in the world of motorsports. At that time Carmelo was directing the construction of the Circuit of Catalunya, having previously directed the building of Calafat circuit, near Tarragona. He was the ROPA representative for Spain and had directed Jarama circuit, just north of Madrid, for ten years.

"It was clear to both the FIM and Dorna that Dorna was in unknown territory," recalls Carmelo. "As soon as we were all back in Spain, I was asked to come and work for Dorna. I thought it over. I had been working with circuits for years. I saw this Dorna offer as a new challenge. I joined Dorna in March 1991 and found myself in a very complicated situation."

Dorna, completely unknown in a tight-knit paddock of players who had worked together for years, inspired no confidence. Whether Ecclestone actually intended to organize a parallel championship or not was immaterial. The doubt created by the menace of a 'World Series' was enough to stymie attempts by Dorna to contract broadcasters and sell sponsorship.

I was working as a GP reporter for Spain's *Solo Moto* at the time. In March 1991, Paul Butler of IRTA arranged for me to have a one-on-one interview with Bernie at his Princes Gate office in London.

Bernie was in a foul mood when I arrived. He had just returned from the Phoenix Formula One Grand Prix and apparently had not enjoyed himself there. "It's not the heat so much as the Americans that he's fed up with," Pasquale Lattunede, one of Bernie's inner circle, told me before Bernie came out and invited me into his office. His desk was a chaos of papers.

The interview began badly when I asked if his interest in Grand Prix motorcycle racing was due to his concern that bike racing might some day be competition for Formula One. His reply was scathing. He said that motorcycle racing would never compete with Formula One. Never, he said, would any form of motorsports, four wheels or two, represent any threat whatsoever to Formula One.

If that were so, I asked, then why become involved in what looked like becoming a battle with the FIM

RIGHT Carmelo Ezpeleta has led the MotoGP revolution from the front.

and Dorna? Why undertake the hard work of organizing a parallel championship?

He explained that he had the full support of the teams, "the IRTA lads", Trimby, Butler, Michel Metraux and Garry Taylor, and enjoyed their confidence. When I asked him if he had met with Dorna, he was evasive, saying only, "They have no one down there who knows anything about motorsport and certainly nothing about motorbike racing."

Then I had the rare opportunity of telling Bernie something that he didn't know about something that directly concerned him.

"That's not altogether true," I said. "They have recently hired Carmelo Ezpeleta."

Bernie's reply baffled me at first. "Carmelo, oh yes. I don't know him as a promoter but he is an excellent jailer. Turn that thing off and let's go outside and discuss this."

Bernie led me out of the front door and we talked in the street. Apparently, all conversations in his office at that time were recorded and moving out into the street may have been a kind of post-Watergate precaution. He was interested to know that Dorna had hired 'a motorsports man' and said he had first known Carmelo when the Formula One Spanish Grand Prix of 1980 was in danger of being cancelled due to a political battle between the Formula One Constructors Association (FOCA), led by Ecclestone, and the Fédération Internationale du Sport Automobile (FISA), the governing body whose President, Jean-Marie Balestre, had suspended the licences of all except the handful of drivers of full factory teams until fines were paid, fines that the FOCA drivers, upon advice from Bernie, were refusing to pay.

"It was all very uncomfortable and the king got involved, as I recall, and gave orders that, no matter what Balestre said, the race had to go on as planned," said Bernie, standing on the pavement in front of Formula One headquarters, the only glass-fronted (one-way reflective glass) structure on a street of otherwise uniform stone and brick buildings of identical height and just off Hyde Park.

"I recall seeing Carmelo instructing members of the Civil Guard to escort FISA officials off the track, at gunpoint, as I recall. I believe they had one poor FISA chap locked up in the back of a police Land Rover. Yes, perhaps Dorna do now have someone who knows how things are done in motorsports."

I had heard a lot about Bernie Ecclestone. That he was witty, brilliant and could charm a cobra. All that seemed true. There was even an office at Princes Gate that the staff called 'the serpent room', where the guest, during negotiations or serious discussions, was seated beneath the gaze of the sculpted figure of a cobra seeming to rise menacingly from a basket.

Meanwhile, back in Spain, Dorna was preparing for battle.

TEETHING PROBLEMS

On the Saturday of the 1991 Spanish Grand Prix at Jerez de la Frontera, the FIM decided to organize a press conference that would serve as Dorna's presentation to the media. President Vaessen hosted and along with him were the executives from Dorna: José Ramón Guimaráes, Carmelo, and the two men in charge of television for the first two years of the Dorna agreement, Jaume Roures and Gerard Romy. The room was small and the journalists were standing. We were packed tight in the room and looming over the FIM and Dorna executives who were seated in low desks, similar to school desks, taken from the press conference area.

Carmelo: "It was the first, official presentation of Dorna to the international press and it was a total disaster right from the beginning."

The press conference had only just begun when the translator, a young Spaniard who spoke a sort of American high school, slangy English, found himself unable to cope with the terminology of contracts, TV rights and championship management. After President Vaessen had paused momentarily as he was explaining the reasons the FIM had decided to accept the Dorna bid, the kid threw up his hands and said, "I can't translate this kind of stuff", and walked out, leaving the FIM President and the four representatives from Dorna sitting there.

"I didn't speak much English back then," recalls Carmelo, "and Guimaráes spoke less than I did, but Romy volunteered to translate and so we went ahead. Vaessen said, in English of course, that the FIM had chosen Dorna because Dorna was a company from outside the world of motorsports and would offer a new perspective. Romy understood what he said but he thought it made no sense for the FIM to choose a company without motorsport experience, so he said the opposite, that, in fact, the FIM had chosen Dorna because Dorna had lots of motorsport experience. The journalists knew that wasn't true and they protested angrily, almost shouting it was a lie, and it just kept getting worse."

While the Spanish and Italian journalists, hearing the translation, were angry that Vaessen had claimed Dorna was a company specialized in motorsports, several English-speaking journalists began to ask questions and were not satisfied with the answers. One of the British journalists had asked an especially aggressive question, basically wondering how Dorna, with no experience in the field, expected to popularize the sport. It was at that point when Dorna's director of television marketing and production, Jaume Roures, sitting aloof at the end of the row of school desks, suddenly slammed his fist on the desktop and shouted, not a word, but a cry of anger and extreme disgust. The journalists, especially the questioner, were taken aback, thinking that perhaps they had hit the limits of Dorna's tolerance. But Roures's sudden outburst had nothing to do with anything happening in Jerez.

In nearby Cadiz and at the Ramón de Carranza stadium, Cadiz had just scored again against Barcelona, taking the score to 3-0. That day Barcelona needed a win to clinch the First Division title. Instead they were humiliated 4-0. It was Saturday, 11 May 1991, an infamous day still recalled by Barcelona fans.

Carmelo: "Roures was paying no attention at all to the press conference. He was listening to the Barcelona-Cadiz game with ear buds via a portable radio in his pocket. Roures was a big Barcelona fan, as I am, and he had no idea what anyone in the room was saying."

Things were very tense. I was wondering if this could get any worse when it suddenly did. José Ramón

ABOVE Before Dorna and the FIM created the GP Safety Commission in 2003, former FIM CCR (Roadrace Commission) Chairman Luigi Brenni was a strong advocate for rider safety. In 1988 IRTA and a large group of top GP riders, past and present, organized a dinner at Assen to thank him for his help on their behalf. Seated to either side of Brenni are (from left) Wayne Gardner, Kenny Roberts, Giacomo Agostini and Carlos Lavado.

RIGHT Dorna´s
successful début
as a GP organizer/
promoter came when
the 1991 Grand Prix
of Yugoslavia was
switched, due to
civil war, from Rijeka
to Jarama in Spain.
Carmelo Ezpeleta: "It
was our opportunity, a
test of fire..."

RIGHT A memento
of that first race — a
basic admission ticket
costing 3,000 pesetas.

Guimaráes (one of the Dorna founders along with Carlos and Manuel García Pardo and José Luis Peña), sitting beside Vaessen, did not like the tone of the questions or the way he believed British journalist Iain Mackay was looking at him. "What is it that you see in my face that you dislike me so much?" asked Guimaráes. "Why are you looking at me like that?" This time Romy translated correctly.

Carmelo: "It was like a scene from a Kafka novel. I looked out at the journalists and saw Spanish magazine owner Jaime Alguersuari making a scissors sign… wanting me to cut the press conference off, but it was already too late."

I was there and I remember one of the other journalists saying that it would take a miracle to get the press to ever take Dorna seriously after that.

In fact, it took a civil war, not in the paddock, but a real and tragic war in Yugoslavia. After the Croatian independence referendum on 19 May 1991, it was clear that there would be war in Yugoslavia, but

Maurizio Flammini, promoter of the Yugoslav Grand Prix scheduled the following month at Rijeka circuit, realized in early spring that he needed a replacement venue. Jarama was chosen.

Carmelo: "This was our opportunity, a test of fire, to show that we knew what we were doing. I had started forming a team by then. You were there working in media. Manel Arroyo, who was still working with the RACC, was there too as was Pep Vila, who was just starting his company, Promotor. Jordi Pons was there coordinating publicity and sponsorship. It was the beginning of the formation of the original Dorna team. And, of course, I had the support of the Jarama staff that I had worked with for many years. It was a successful event."

The event, held on 16 June, went well. Dorna's reputation was much improved after the European Grand Prix at Jarama, but there were problems on the horizon. The immediate task was to avoid the threat of an Ecclestone-organized 'World Series' with the top teams and riders.

FROM JARAMA TO CATALUNYA TO CHRISTCHURCH TO LONDON

Carmelo Ezpeleta recalls the situation as the 1991 season moved along. "We had gained some credibility after we organized the European Grand Prix at Jarama as a replacement for Yugoslavia, but I knew that Bernie was strengthening his position with IRTA and the circuits. We met him in London and I told him that we needed to find a better way to avoid confrontation and it really didn't take us long to come to an agreement to work together, but now we had to convince our partners to cooperate."

By then it was September 1991 and Ecclestone only needed IRTA to procure sufficient agreements with teams to allow TWP to negotiate from a position of strength with the FIM and Dorna.

Carmelo and Richard Golding, Dorna's original Managing Director, met with the FIM on 21 and 22 September and told the members of the management council that if they did not accept an agreement between all the parties — FIM, Dorna, TWP and IRTA — Ecclestone and IRTA were going to run a parallel series with all the best teams and riders.

The FIM were opposed at first but they finally agreed to a meeting between Vaessen, Ecclestone and Dorna during the Formula One Spanish Grand Prix at the Circuit of Catalunya on the last weekend of September, the same weekend as the motorcycle Grand Prix in Shah Alam, Malaysia.

Manel Arroyo had not yet joined Dorna. It was at the Formula One Spanish Grand Prix in 1991, the inaugural World Championship event at the new Catalonian circuit, that Manel first found himself involved in the preliminary stages of the long and complicated negotiations that would eventually avoid the possibility of parallel FIM and 'World Series' championships.

Manel Arroyo: "I was in the midst of my duties as Press Officer for the F1 race, but at the same time, there were a series of meetings being held in Bernie's paddock office. At the end of my day dealing with F1 responsibilities, I found myself transcribing documents and contracts that had been drafted during meetings between Dorna, Bernie and FIM President Jos Vaessen. It was an exciting, emotional weekend. The future of Grand Prix motorcycle road racing was being decided and I had already agreed with Carmelo to join Dorna. I was going to be a part of that world."

Mike Trimby adds an important detail: "We knew Bernie was meeting with the FIM and Dorna in Barcelona and we knew he needed IRTA to get an agreement with Yamaha signed in Shah Alam. I called Bernie at the Circuit of Catalunya and told him Yamaha had signed, so he met with the FIM and Dorna knowing that he now had the proportion of teams required in the pre-agreement between TWP and IRTA. Now he could negotiate reconciliation."

After what was called 'the Barcelona agreement', Vaessen had 30 days to get the approval of the management council. He left Barcelona confident that he could convince the Management Council, so confident that the FIM office put out a press release on September 29, the same Sunday the papers were signed, affirming an agreement between the FIM, Dorna, IRTA and TWP. IRTA put out a similar release announcing that this agreement enabled it "to reach its objectives without leaving the FIM orbit".

But at the nadir of that FIM orbit, in Christchurch, New Zealand, site of the 1991 FIM Congress, the agreement was rejected. Zerbi was quoted as expressing "dismay" at the conditions and Wilhelm Noll, a Vice President, called the agreement "a declaration of failure". Vaessen said he had no alternative, given the discontent of the council, but to recommend, in the name of the Management Council, that the general assembly reject 'the Barcelona agreement'.

TWP and Dorna were shocked by the reversal. They both had been especially confident after an additional meeting between the parties was held at Heathrow airport, London, on 15 October, just before the FIM President left for New Zealand.

Once again, a parallel championship seemed imminent and this time Dorna was on the side of the rebels. The agreement that Dorna had reached with the FIM had never actually committed the FIM legally but, with the express understanding that FIM approval would be a formality, Dorna had signed a binding agreement with TWP. Now the FIM was completely alone and it looked as if Dorna would join TWP in organizing what the FIM would consider an 'outlaw' championship.

When the FIM executives and delegates returned home, they were bombarded with criticism, especially from circuit owners and race promoters. How could a circuit hope to promote an FIM Grand Prix with no guarantee that any of the top riders would compete? On the other hand, how could a circuit agree to host a 'pirate' event knowing that doing so would mean that the FIM would not sanction any other events at the venue? It was an impossible situation.

Claudio Castiglioni, the owner of Cagiva, stepped in as peacemaker and got the FIM executives to sit down once again with TWP and Dorna. On 15 November 1991, an FIM delegation including Vaessen, Zerbi, CCR President Joseph Zegwaard and General Secretary Guy Maitre met with Ecclestone, Ezpeleta and Golding in London. TWP and Dorna were now united and in a strong enough position to insist on adding to the original Barcelona agreement the rights to make the schedule and contract the circuits and promoters. More importantly, the new contract went into immediate effect in 1992 rather than 1993. By the time the contract was finally signed and the 1992 schedule announced on 28 February, the first race of the new era was less than a month away.

THE 'DORNA DOZEN'

Manel Arroyo remembers that that month passed very quickly as Dorna prepared to share with TWP and the FIM the responsibility of running a world championship. "Suddenly it was March and we were in Japan, a small group of us, a dozen. We were so few that all

RIGHT Manel Arroyo's drive and foresight has brought live MotoGP pictures to millions of television viewers world-wide.

ABOVE The Dorna era of GP racing began on 29 March 1992 at the rainy Japanese Grand Prix. The race winners were Honda riders — Mick Doohan in 500, Luca Cadalora in 250 and Ralf Waldmann in 125. Here Cadalora leads third-placed Nobuatsu Aoki.

RIGHT The 1992 FIM Grand Prix season was run under shared management by Dorna and Bernie Ecclestone's company Two Wheel Promotions.

of us had dinner together at the same table at the hotel — Carmelo's Dorna dozen. My memories of that time are that we really didn't know what we were supposed to do. I can't lie. It was like my first day on the job as Press Officer for the RAC, but much bigger and we were in Suzuka, in the midst of an enormous event… there was the federation, IRTA, the factories, the Suzuka promoter, and we were supposed to be in charge of all that! And all of it against a terrible background of rain and wind and cold, the traditional setting for the Japanese Grand Prix! I remember our offices were stuck away in a commentary booth on the far side of the track and every time we had a meeting we had to go from one side of the circuit to the other. We didn't even have a copy of the promoter's contract; only Bernie had that, so we weren't even sure of what rights we had. It was terrible!"

Terribly hectic too. I was Press Officer for the series and I don't think I was ever in the Media Centre for more than a few minutes at a time. There was too much to do and no time to be hanging around my office. I remember, vaguely, a call at dawn in Japan from someone who never identified himself. He asked, "Did you book the satellite?" Was I supposed to? "Well, someone was supposed to." I guess someone did because the race was televised.

It was a rough beginning. The opening rounds were a trio of 'fly-aways' in Japan, Australia and Malaysia — 'the War of the Pacific' we called it — but by the time we got to round seven at Hockenheim for the German Grand Prix we had found our feet.

There were two dozen of us by then and we were all learning on the job, learning from the experts at IRTA and from the FIM stewards and helpful team bosses.

At paddock level, with racing engines roaring in the background, we were all on the same team, but in the offices there were still disputed commercial issues. At every Grand Prix time was spent trying to sort out conflicts between TWP contracts and Dorna contracts for everything from hospitality and signage to passes and parking. Then, at Donington, Carmelo and Bernie had a long talk.

"This was the year of the Olympics in Barcelona," recalls Carmelo. "Our first season was almost over. We were at Donington Park for the British Grand Prix, round 11 of 13, during the first week of the Barcelona Olympics. Bernie and I sat down together in the Wheatcroft House at the end of the Donington home straight. It had been a long day, discussing passes and other details with Gardella, the Race Director. There had been tension and disagreements that day and at other circuits too. I complained about this and Bernie said, 'This business we have got ourselves into is very complicated and I just don't delegate, but I can't attend all the races either. So we have a problem. I suggest we decide what this whole thing is worth and either I buy your 50 per cent off you or you buy my 50 per cent off me.' He went on to say that he'd rather sell and I said that was good because I'd rather buy, but that I'd have to get approval from Madrid. I got the approval and we bought Two Wheel Promotions with all its rights and contracts."

For Dorna, this opportunity came at a difficult time due to Banesto, owner of 50 per cent of Dorna, having encountered financial difficulties during this period of recession. Dorna, however, was able to obtain the necessary loan from the Central Bank of Spain. As part of the purchase of TWP by Dorna, there was an agreement that Dorna would avoid television scheduling conflicts with Formula One, an agreement beneficial to both parties. Dorna finally had not only the rights they had sought since 1990, but a complete commercial rights package and a seat at the table with the FIM regarding sporting and technical regulations. With the rights to contract circuits, Dorna now shared overall authority with the FIM… so much more than was bid for that day back in Budapest. The Dorna/IRTA/FIM structure, established after the purchase of TWP, remains firm to this day, but there would be unexpected problems.

BANKS, CONSPIRACY AND SUPERBIKES TOO

While the racing roared round us, there were still battles being fought in the paddock and the offices. As Dorna worked through the first full year as exclusive commercial and TV rights holder, Banesto was on the brink of insolvency and, on 28 December 1993,

the Bank of Spain put it into receivership. A year later the Santander Group bought Banesto and, in 1995, instructed Banesto to sell all holdings that were not strictly related to banking.

Carmelo: "When Santander ordered the sale of all the non-banking properties, Maurizio Flammini with backing from Tommy Suharto, a son of the President of Indonesia, made an offer and so did a few other companies."

Once again Dorna was on the trading block and there were several bidders, among them IMG from the US, The Ogden Group from the UK and Spain's broadcasting and publishing giant, Prisa. Then there was a bad surprise.

Carmelo: "Some call it the IRTA Conspiracy. While we were at work preparing for the 1996 season, the IRTA pre-season tests were taking place in Jerez and the IRTA officials, Michel Metraux, Sito Pons and Mike Trimby, the President, Vice President and General Secretary, called a press conference in Jerez at the track and announced that, because Dorna, they alleged, had not fulfilled all obligations to IRTA, they had signed a new agreement with ISL (International Sports and Leisure) and that ISL was going to draw up the calendar, contract circuits and organize the championship."

According to Mike Trimby, Metraux and ROC Yamaha team owner Serge Rosset unilaterally started discussions with the French subsidiary of ISL Switzerland. ISL France was represented in the talks by ex-racer Christian Leliard. All this was unbeknownst at

LEFT At the 1992 British Grand Prix at Donington Park, Carmelo Ezpeleta and Bernie Ecclestone met and agreed that Dorna would buy all rights and contracts from TWP.

ABOVE **IRTA founder Mike Trimby outside his new office during the 1987 Japanese Grand Prix at Suzuka.**

BELOW **Orderly parking of motorhomes in the 1992 Hungarian Grand Prix paddock.**

their minds were made up, but it's easy to see now that the deal with ISL France was never, ever going to work. I recall we announced it at Jerez at the IRTA test prior to the 1996 season, which was the last year of the IRTA/Dorna contract of that time. The whole ISL deal was scuppered the moment Bernie got involved and I thought IRTA was finished."

Carmelo: "We had worked with Ecclestone for the entire 1992 season and, after we bought TWP, our relations were good and we stayed in touch. Ecclestone flew down to Madrid and we discussed a strategy. While IRTA and ISL were still trying to create their own championship, Ecclestone and I met with Santiago Zaldumbide, the CEO of the Banesto Corporation, and I told Santiago that Bernie was prepared to buy Dorna's rights, guaranteeing a yearly fee to the corporation. Bernie and I then met with the new FIM President, Francesco Zerbi, and we signed an agreement at Barajas airport, Madrid before flying to Jerez during the Spanish Grand Prix, where we announced the new plan.

"When Flammini heard about this, he said it was terrible and that it could not be allowed. His next move was to meet with Banesto. He said that he, not Ecclestone, would buy Dorna and that he had a partner, Tommy Suharto, and that Banesto didn't need Ecclestone's guarantees because Tommy Suharto and he would buy it all. When Ecclestone heard this, he was furious. Flammini, now believing he was going to buy Dorna, planned a visit to the Dorna offices to have a look at the books. That was when I went to Zaldumbide and said that we couldn't show our internal accounts because, if Flammini backed out, he'd have seen the internals, the guts, of all our contracts, much of it confidential between Dorna and third parties, and all of it vital information to us.

"That angered Flammini but he returned to Banesto and, seemingly confident of his support from Suharto, made an offer to pay Banesto annually out of profits from the running of the series, which was the same as leveraging the whole purchase and not paying anything except what the championship itself generated. Zaldumbide replied, 'That seems fine as long as you guarantee these payments.' I remember that Flammini's reply was, 'How can you ask for a bank guarantee from one of the richest men in the world?' To which Zaldumbide answered, 'Well, precisely because he is one of the richest men in the world he'll have no problem giving this guarantee.'

"And there it all broke down. There was no guarantee, no nothing. They didn't buy. There was a lot of controversy and finally I suggested to Zaldumbide that it would be better to allow Dorna to consolidate before putting it up for sale. 'Give us two or three

first to Dorna, but when Mark McCormack, frustrated in his attempts to acquire TV rights in 1990, heard that IRTA was discussing a new break-away attempt, he sent IMG representatives to Geneva to make a last-minute pitch at an IRTA committee meeting. By then, however, an agreement had already been made with ISL France. Dorna learned of this prior to the Jerez IRTA tests and Ecclestone once again became involved, this time on behalf of Dorna's management.

Mike Trimby: "Michel and Serge were committed;

years for the company to stabilize and then if you want to sell, sell.' And that is what he did.

"IRTA and ISL never managed to put a plan together and the person who had signed the deal with IRTA for ISL took IRTA to court and won a financial settlement. But all this created uncertainty in the paddock, especially since IRTA was still functioning in spite of the attempt to join forces with ISL to form a new series."

Manel Arroyo recalls: "The IRTA-ISL situation came to a head on Thursday, 4 April, at the 1996 Indonesian Grand Prix. We were at breakfast when we received word from our lawyers in Madrid. They sent us, by fax in those days, a racing calendar that they had published without the knowledge of the majority of circuit owners. That was too much. The game was over."

Throughout the spring there continued to be rumours and doubts, but it was soon clear that the ISL-IRTA attempt had failed completely. The factories, teams, circuits and sponsors all wanted stability. I asked Carmelo how it was that, after all that had happened; he decided to continue to work with IRTA.

"I considered IRTA, the people who worked in IRTA, to be competent and I needed a competent team organization," says Carmelo, "but I also considered all their leaders to be equally guilty for the conspiracy so I decided we could make a change of leadership and then continue. We could not have IRTA led by the identical team that had attempted all that, so we continued, but with a new President. It was, to be precise, our decision, Dorna's decision, to continue working with IRTA. Some people left IRTA, among them the President, but after this incident, we began to work much more closely with IRTA and all the organizations that make up our paddock and our sport. It was really the beginning of the application of rule by consensus, of racing and deciding together. That unity has been the key to out success — consulting each other and listening to each other."

I recall that Santiago Zaldumbide travelled to the Czech Republic and met with the FIM and team owners, telling them that Dorna was stable and that there was no imminent sale. After several years of turmoil and rumours in the motorcycling press, attention was turned back to the racing itself. Instead of wondering who would manage Grand Prix racing, journalists asked if European riders would ever overcome the mid-nineties Japanese dominance in 125cc (a young Italian named Rossi would break the Japanese stronghold), if Max Biaggi would continue his string of titles in 250cc (he would win four in a row before moving to 500), and if Yamaha and Suzuki would find a way of curtailing the Honda monopoly in 500cc (after six consecutive 500 titles, Honda lost to Kenny Roberts Jr and Suzuki in 2000).

Then, in 1998, Dorna was finally sold.

Carmelo: "In 1998, CVC Capital Partners came along. They wanted to undertake a management buy-out and I didn't even know what that was. They wanted to know how much capital we had and if we believed in our own company enough to invest in a buy-out. We certainly believed in what we were doing and we were able, together with CVC, to buy Dorna from Banesto in 1998."

This situation continued until CVC proposed to buy Formula One. The European Commission saw a conflict and CVC, facing a time limit on the Formula One purchase, agreed to divest completely of all interests in Dorna and eventually sold its holdings to Bridgepoint Capital in 2006. In 2012, Canadian Pension Plan acquired 39 per cent of Bridgepoint's Dorna holdings. Coincidentally, among the many properties managed or owned by Infront was the World Superbike Championship!

Carmelo: "World Superbike had been bought and sold many times since Steve McLaughlin and his New Zealand partners founded it in 1988. When Bridgepoint bought Infront, the sports marketing company that owned World Superbike, their idea was for the two motorcycle championships to be run separately but, after a series of very long meetings to try and avoid conflicts, Bridgepoint lost patience and turned Superbikes over to us. Now it's our responsibility to develop SBK as it was originally intended to be: the world's second most important motorcycle racing championship and the world's only series for motorcycles derived from production models. We are determined to develop the SBK Championship to its maximum potential and we will do that."

RIGHT Mike Trimby is the cornerstone of IRTA and the MotoGP revolution.

CHAPTER 2
A PERSONAL DORNA JOURNEY
BY IGNACIO SAGNIER

A lot has happened since the days when I would try, at times with more success than others, to sneak into the Grand Prix paddocks and other races and events where the smell of petrol was ever-present. I was still short when, with my Dad, I went down to a windy Calafat circuit — whose construction was initiated by Dorna CEO Carmelo Ezpeleta — to go to the 'Superprestigio'. Then, it was an exhibition race that *Solo Moto* magazine organised as a season closer, and it came to be very popular with fans. We would all wait for the date of the 'Superprestigio' to be announced so we could put it in our diaries, and take note of the list of riders who would be lining up.

At the end of the eighties and in the early nineties,

it was a must to head down to the Tarragona circuit to get a look at some of the biggest stars of the time: Aspar, Crivillé, Pons, Gresini, Kocinski, Garriga, Raudies or even Wimmer all made it a date to remember at the end of the year, and at a place that allowed you to see them up close. That smell of petrol was like a drug, and to me it will always be intertwined with Calafat and that 'Superprestigio' race from another era. An era it was; the Superprestigio in 1986 was the final race of the late, great Ángel Nieto, the event in which he broke his knee.

But fans would head to Calafat only until 1990, which is when the 'Superprestigio' moved to Barcelona on a much improved and safer stage, and as the

BELOW The paddock at Mugello in 1993 with the Dorna fleet.

first race on two wheels organised at the newly inaugurated Circuit de Catalunya. And it was Carmelo Ezpeleta, now CEO of Dorna, who oversaw the construction of the venue up until March 1991. It was a big project, and one he only left in order to join Dorna — just months before the ribbon was cut on the new track. It was then inaugurated on 10 September 1991 with a Spanish Touring Car Championship race, and took over from the legendary street circuit of Montjuïc that was no longer on the FIM calendar. The first race on two wheels at the Circuit de Catalunya took place the following month.

Dorna, as Dennis Noyes explains in the previous chapter, has always been linked to Catalonian, Spanish and world motorcycling — with some of the top people in the company having been part of this world since that first motorcycle race at the Circuit de Catalunya, a day that serves to better explain and introduce the story of Dorna. Within the team of organisers were Manel Arroyo and Jordi Pons, who already worked for the circuit and the RACC (Royal Automobile Club of Catalonia). Arroyo, the current Director of the TV and Media Area at Dorna, and Pons, one of the first Commercial Directors, would then leave the RACC and the circuit to join Dorna, where they found themselves in one of the best showcases in the world.

Pons joined Dorna in October 1991, with Arroyo coming on board a month later. The former left the RACC just after the first Formula One Grand Prix held

LEFT Jordi Pons (left), here with Pep Vila, was one of Dorna's pioneers in 1991.

at the Circuit de Catalunya on 29 September 1991, whereas the latter waited another month in order to finish organising the Rally of Catalunya — part of the World Rally Championship and something that has always been close to Arroyo, a former organiser, co-pilot and native of Vic, which the Rally went through.

BELOW The same paddock 24 years later, with Dorna offices prominent.

RIGHT The start of the
TV revolution with the
original editing studio
and transmission bus at
San Marino in 1993.

BELOW The TV nerve
centre, the 2017 IPF,
which directs all world-
wide broadcasting.

"Carmelo called us — he'd been our boss at the circuit — and asked us to go with him into motorbikes. We said yes," remembers Pons, whose first job at Dorna was Commercial Director. Thereafter it was Marketing and then Operations, before he left in 2002 when Managing Director of the FIM Motocross World Championship, for which Dorna had acquired the rights — as well as those of the CEV. But his fingerprint and way of doing things have remained within the company. "I remember thinking that what we did was completely impulsive. We had everything: a stable job with the RACC with a good future, the WRC in Catalonia,

and the return of F1 after many years. We were in a privileged position and the call from Dorna was an adventure into the unknown.

"At the time we didn't know anything about bikes, but the call from Carmelo was very real and we threw ourselves into it. Like I said, working for the RACC was everyone's dream, and we left that behind for Dorna. I remember for the first Christmas meal in 1991, Manel and I went to Madrid and went into this restaurant where there were 100 people we didn't know — and we looked at each other and asked ourselves what we'd got ourselves into! It was a strange feeling, but youth and the desire to *do* outweighed everything."

In 2005, Pons would leave Dorna to pursue his own projects for three years and after returning now holds the reins of Promomedia, a sporting agency that helps to organise championships searching for new talents on the Road to MotoGP: the Red Bull MotoGP Rookies Cup for the energy drinks giant, the Asia Talent Cup, the Asia Talent Team, the British Talent Team and the British Talent Cup, the last of which begins in 2018.

"Dorna has been the best girlfriend I could ever have had, the perfect partner," says Pons. And he picks out the work of some colleagues in particular: Carmelo, Manel, Alberto Puig, Pep Vila and his wife Rosa Ars. Pons recognises that Puig has been — and will continue to be — a key figure in the discovery of new talents, after having also contributed to the creation of the Movistar Cup that discovered riders such as Pedrosa and Stoner: "Casey we went looking for in England,"

he remembers with satisfaction, "after we were told that there was this Australian kid *flying* on track!"

From 1991, three years before the 'Doohan era', my passion for two wheels kept growing. Grand Prix after Grand Prix. Getting up at dawn for the races in Asia because what counts is watching live and in the moment, not a retransmission of what has already happened. Then watching the mythical Australian win and win as I prepared to go and work in the US. To be precise, I was headed for the Olympics in Atlanta in 1996 — the year when Enrique Aldama became non-executive president of Dorna, taking the first step on a journey that would see him take the reins of the company's finances.

Back then, Aldama was the Business Director of the Banesto Corporation. In 1990, Banesto had bought 50% of Dorna Sports Promotion from Carlos Garcia Pardo, who was head of the Dorna Group. It was a group that began with a construction company. Aldama frames that time within the frantic evolution of buying sports rights — before they would go on to become the everyday bread and butter of the company: "Carlos had many different businesses and companies. For some reason, he named this one after a type of Galician fishing boat…"

In 1993, scandal hit Banesto and it was taken over by the Bank of Spain — news that had a big impact both within the country and globally. Dorna Promoción del Deporte, which was owned by that entity, continued to operate normally, but financing having come from Banesto meant the arena had changed. In May 1996, Banesto then acquired 100% of Dorna — and that's when Enrique Aldama joined. There was a change of board, and Aldama was named Non-Executive President, meaning that he watched what happened within the company, but didn't work within it.

"I met Carmelo in 1995 and Manel and Pons a year later," remembers Aldama. "When I arrived as President, I soon realised there were professional people there who knew what they were doing, which made me feel calmer. In 1996, Dorna's main job was organising the Motorcycle World Championship, but they knew they needed someone to oversee the financial, legal and economic side of the company. That's when I came on board."

The year 1998 brought a key moment for Dorna. An agreement was made with venture capital fund CVC for 100% of the company, which was when Aldama then left as President. The arrival of CVC stabilised Dorna: before then, the team weren't able to look further ahead than the season underway — and avoided selling the company to an international corporation or investment fund lest they decide to begin again with new people or in another country. But just six months after the sale, new owners CVC and Dorna CEO Carmelo Ezpeleta approached Aldama to ask if he would be interested in returning, this time running the finances and business aspects of the company — creating a new chapter in the story. He joined Dorna as an employee and was involved in the decision making for the first time in early 1999.

Aldama has good memories of the beginning of that new chapter: "I would highlight how we were able to create a company that until then had never acted as such. There were different departments that worked, but it needed a management committee to decide on which steps to take and to focus on only the World Championship — before they organised concerts, football… things that were sometimes a distraction."

Aldama decided to make the most of the expertise of the people in the company — and each decision that was taken. This helped the company grow and at the same time become a bigger fish within the world of motorcycling.

One of the other most important steps forward within the company in the first few years was another noteworthy evolution: "The changes in media, and the vision to change the sale of collective television rights to a more individualised system, country by country." That was undoubtedly a clear aim of the directors of the company, as the championship grew and allowed the individual sale of rights that hadn't been possible before, improving both performance and audiences.

Another important moment was when CVC bought the rights to Formula One. The EU considered that to be risking a monopoly if one company controlled both championships, and the European Competition Network forced CVC to sell their interests in Dorna. Bridgepoint bought it in 2006 and demanded more involvement. Then Canadian fund

RIGHT Enrique Aldama, Dorna COO, joined the company in 1999 and has played a major part in its strategy.

ABOVE The first Dorna
fleet, in 1994 in France.

CPPIB arrived in 2013 and consolidated the strategy of the shareholders. That was when Dorna opted for growth by means of acquisition and purchased the FIM Superbike World Championship, WorldSBK, making Dorna the strongest company within the world panorama of short-circuit racing.

Aldama finishes his reminiscences with a message on the future: "Since 2013 we have been focusing on growing and developing the championships we are involved in, giving maximum priority to obtaining talent through the cups we organise or supporting other initiatives around the world. This is with the aim of

growing our sport in continents such as Asia and the Americas.

"Objectives are always reached by the people within a company, and the initial team at Dorna has meant that it has been able to grow and evolve. When I joined in 1996, I could see that the fusion of motorcycling to the passion of the people there would allow us to elevate this sport and the company to the incredible levels we see now in 2017."

The great relationship between Aldama and Ezpeleta stems from "understanding each other, and knowing what the other is thinking with just a look". Aldama

RIGHT Enjoying MotoGP
VIP Village privileges at
Jerez in 2017.

also adds that "if you grow a lot but without keeping control of it, things can get away from you."

Returning from Aldama to Jordi Pons, the man who opens this chapter, he was responsible for contracting the Managing Director of the Commercial Area, Pau Serracanta, in February 1999. That year was an important one for Dorna as it also saw another important name, Javier Alonso, known as 'Yupi' in MotoGP, join the company alongside Serracanta and Aldama.

Alonso has been another important figure during this journey. He started as a member of the Promotor team before moving to Dorna, where he went on to become Managing Director of Events, as well as a member of Race Direction until he left the company at the end of 2016. Amongst other things, 'Yupi' was the person who furthered links between Dorna and promotors across the world and was in charge of circuit homologation prior to FIM giving its go-ahead. He also liaised with the riders, teams and organisations that form this world — like IRTA or the MSMA.

Pau Serracanta, on the other hand, entered the company as Head of Sales. Two years later he was named Commercial Director, before moving up to Managing Commercial Director in 2004: "When I arrived at Dorna, there were three important challenges facing us. The first was working on the brand to make MotoGP a commercially viable sale. The second was to create a sales strategy via agents for whom workshops in Barcelona were created. The third was to prepare — from a commercial standpoint — for the post-tobacco era that was on the horizon by 2006. We knew those sponsors would disappear within seven years and we had to find new ways of filling the gap. But the disappearance of tobacco sponsorship opened doors to other opportunities with different brands. We had to diversify into other products such as airlines, energy drinks, 360 packages, hospitality programmes, B2B experiences. You could say that's when we became pioneers into the 21st century."

After Serracanta's arrival, Dorna opened up new commercial avenues and now stands firmly on more than solid ground. The MotoGP VIP Village is a reference in the sector, and the Licensing department has 70 licences with more than 1,800 products. Serracanta has a clear vision of the future of Dorna: "The world championship for electric bikes in 2019, Moto-E, and eSports, will play a big role. Growth is important. But we are in good health with a title sponsor for every race." He also points out the incredible loyalty of the fans — and those brands that have been partners for a long time such as Freixenet, BMW, Tissot and Phillip Morris.

Since the beginnings of Dorna, in a Barcelona yet to host the Olympics, there are also a handful of people who have remained under the umbrella of the company. Vicente Jimenez is one such figure; a man who joined Dorna S.A. at the end of 1977 when he was only 16 and Dorna was focused on estate agency management. His career went on to develop throughout different companies in the group — first in property, then film production (Asterisco Films S.A.), then sports promotion; the forerunner to Dorna Sports that began representing athletes and later purchased the commercial rights to FC Barcelona, Real Madrid and other teams in *La Liga*. In other words, Jimenez has spent a lifetime with the company.

There's also Sergi Sendra, who joined in February 1992 as a television cameraman and was one of the brave men who débuted in the Japanese Grand Prix that year at Suzuka — the first one organised by Dorna. Now, Sergi is the Director of the TV Department, managing the direction and production of MotoGP coverage beamed to millions around the world, and has been a key figure in the development of this technical area. Arroyo's aim was to create a consistent feed for all GPs and this was perfectly implemented by Sendra. From the first version of the IPF (International Programme Feed) at the 1996 Japanese Grand Prix to now, he has been a driving force behind the evolution of the MotoGP broadcast, putting together the teams and technology allowing for unprecedented onboard camera coverage, state-of-the-art graphics and 360 imagery — amongst many other innovations. This founding group also includes Amparo Porto who joined in January 1992 as Carmelo Ezpeleta's PA and now leads the Talent Promotion Department while also looking after the contractual relationships with circuit promoters. Pilar Gancedo moved from Antena3 TV in 1994 to lead the commercial side of the media area, which underwent intense evolution and

RIGHT Pau Serracanta, Managing Director at Dorna, defines the company's commercial strategy.

ABOVE What a contrast: pre-event preparations at Malaysia, Johor Bahru in 1998 and Austria's Red Bull Ring in 2017.

RIGHT Sergi Sendra at Brno in 1993. From cameraman to TV master, he has raised broadcasting quality to another level, where MotoGP production is a benchmark for all.

the passion for the sport — without that, it's impossible to survive in this world.

Passion is what — once more with my dad — led me down to see the start of the Dakar Rally on a frosty Christmas morning in Barcelona in 1988. The RACC organised it, with Ezpeleta, Arroyo and Pons working on their first major project together. It was an exhibition stage stopping off in Barcelona before arriving on African territory that Pep Vila was already working on. Vila at the time was working with Promotor, a company he founded that same year and one that's another important cornerstone in the story of Dorna.

The huge logistical operation required by Dorna nowadays is directed from a giant warehouse in Callús, in the centre of Catalonia, by Pep Vila and his crew. Vila is another of these mythical figures who had already collaborated with Ezpeleta, Arroyo and Pons 25 years ago when they worked for the RACC. The Promotor guys are the gladiators of MotoGP, the ones who spend so much time away from home without a single complaint, unrelenting workhorses whose contributions go out across the world on TV, and who make life so much easier for the people working in the paddock as they move from place to place.

Pep Vila remembers the journey with perfect clarity: "We were and in many ways still are like the hands of the RACC because now I have 60 people in the Rally of Catalunya, but the time with Dorna has been memorable and we always dedicate ourselves to it 100% — heart and soul." His company first worked on the Rally of Catalonia, and after came the Camel

change in parallel with steady growth. Eugeni de Haro did the same in 2000 after eight years as a freelance contractor — his first race was Jerez in 1992 — and Albert Del Diestro is another name to add. After working at the 1992 Olympics, he joined Dorna in 1997 and is now Office Director in Barcelona.

For someone like me, who has been passionate about bikes for so long, Dorna has always been a point of reference. Something more than 'the bike company'. "It's a Spanish company who does this, not British or American?" is the question people always ask!

I joined Dorna in February 2011, after covering MotoGP for two years for Diario SPORT — years I'd spent, at times, interviewing the people who would then become my bosses. The possibility of joining arose through pure chance, and since then I've tried to enjoy every minute of every day.

Sometimes it may have been four days, but it feels like it must have been decades. When you spend more time on planes than on your own sofa, you barely have time to appreciate the details. But time flies thanks to

Trophy, the Baja Aragón and then the Dakar, as well as the organization of the torch relay for the Barcelona Olympics — and finally the world of motorcycle racing. At the Japanese Grand Prix in 2017, Vila reached the milestone of 400 GPs.

The Grand Prix run at Jarama in 1991, when the track was the substitute venue for Yugoslavia due to the Balkan war, was the first time Promotor came into contact with motorcycle Grand Prix racing. The request came from Carmelo, who asked for their help, and Promotor were here to stay. At first they dealt with the circuit advertising and it began a relationship that continues in good health to this day. Back then, Promotor was a group of only four, but has now grown into a fixed group of 30 that can expand to a staff of 80 at particularly demanding moments of the season.

Pep, a truck driver who has finished 12 of the 13 Dakar Rallies he has entered, and is a five-times Spanish Enduro and Raids Champion, says there is a clear thing in common across the management of both Promotor and Dorna: "We're people who know what it is to race and to put on a helmet. At Dorna, that's true of key people in the management."

Carles Jorba, who joined Dorna in 2000 and is now Senior Operations Director, is another who began at Promotor in 1991 alongside Vila and Alonso, driving trucks and installing advertisement hoardings at circuits. Those times at Promotor were tough but memorable. Only four vehicles and two scooters travelled with all the equipment, something that seems a distant memory compared with the 18 trucks and 20 scooters that travel today — and that's not including the safety cars.

The passion of the people involved in Dorna, MotoGP and motorcycle racing is the constant thread woven into each year and season that passes. From small beginnings to an incredible vision of the future, the evolution I have watched first from afar and then within has a simple but powerful force behind it: the people who, like me, have their own memories conjured up by that mythical smell of petrol. Whether it be the 'Superprestigio' at Calafat or, for the coming generation, the event by the same name at the Palau Sant Jordi, passion will always be the common thread and the means by which the sport and the company will continue to evolve. As I said, time flies thanks to the passion we all share — and the past 25 years seem to have done just that.

ABOVE Some Dorna and Promotor pioneers in Brazil. Among them are Manel Arroyo (check shirt), Carlos Jorba (white T-shirt) and Cesc and Pep Vila (right).

BELOW The complete Promotor team at Brno in 2017 — they are a vital part of MotoGP success.

CHAPTER 3
THE QUEST FOR IMPROVEMENT
BY DENNIS NOYES

SAFETY: THE MAN WITH THE $10,000 FOOTSTEP

Our paddock is a tight community, as intimate as a small town, diverse but unified, and all are aware of the need to constantly improve safety while accepting the realities of motorcycle racing.

After the tragic accident of Daijiro Kato during the 2003 Japanese Grand Prix at Suzuka, the Grand Prix Safety Commission was formed at the following South African Grand Prix. The Safety Commission, open to all riders, now meets on Friday afternoon after practice at every Grand Prix and is normally attended by all the top MotoGP riders. There riders express their concerns over all matters having to do with safety, from run-off area

and curbing to technical details (like brake disc diameter and aerodynamics) and even rider on-track conduct.

From the beginning of this quarter century of cooperation between the FIM, IRTA, the MSMA and Dorna, safety has been the overriding concern. This has meant that some grand old circuits, rich in tradition, have lost their place on the calendar because they cannot, for any number of reasons, be brought up to the latest and constantly evolving standards.

In the early days of Dorna, I accompanied IRTA's Franco Uncini, the 1982 500cc World Champion, and the FIM's Claude Danis on safety inspections of American circuits. Dorna wanted very much to continue in the United States, but only 13,000 fans attended the United States Grand Prix at Laguna Seca on race day in 1994, about the same as the year before. The Laguna Seca promoter, SCRAMP, a non-profit organization, could not continue at the time. Other tracks were interested but Uncini and Danis were uncompromising. I remember the then director of Road America in Wisconsin called Uncini "the man with the $10,000 footstep" because each pace he made when marking off additional run-off area was that expensive… or more!

At beautiful Road America in Wisconsin there was only one really insurmountable problem: a quick right-hander with a very large, rocky hill on the right and a railroad line on left, where the run-off should have been.

The circuit director, Uncini, Danis and I were out at the corner in question on a snowy, winter morning. The circuit director believed that a problem on only one of the many corners "could be gotten around".

"How?" Uncini asked. The circuit director thought for a while. "Well," he said hopefully, "we could put in a speed limit here, make it a neutralized zone."

Uncini seemed to consider that briefly and then said: "I see three solutions and that is not one of them. One: move the railroad. Two: move the hill. Three: move the track." He then began pacing off a variant that involved

BELOW Following the tragic death of Daijiro Kato in the 2003 Japanese Grand Prix at Suzuka, the Grand Prix Safety Commission was formed.

ABOVE With safety becoming a heightened concern in 2003, Sete Gibernau, Nobuatsu Aoki and Valentino Rossi have deep discussion at that year's South African Grand Prix.

LEFT The man with the $10,000 footstep, and the BMW Safety Car, is Franco Uncini, 1982 500cc World Champion and now FIM Safety Officer for MotoGP.

reversing the direction of racing from clockwise to counter clockwise and increasing run-off room at almost every corner. Danis followed, writing in his notebook.

That day Franco Uncini, the man with the $10,000 footstep, paced off what the circuit owner estimated in millions of dollars. I remember his footprints in the Wisconsin snow.

Safety matters never remain constant. Today's MotoGP 1,000cc bikes are over 40km/h faster than the old 500s at the end of the long home straights at Mugello and the Circuit of Catalunya, and advances in electronics, tyres, aerodynamics, chassis and suspension have increased corner speeds everywhere. Old newsreel footage of the classic battles of the sixties and seventies reveal realities of those times… naked steel barriers, stone walls, even the railroad crossing at Imatra, Finland.

Once circuits were built with automobiles in mind and motorcycles were an afterthought. Kel Carruthers, 1969 250cc World Champion on a four-cylinder Benelli, once told me, "If you wanted to be fast in my day you never looked beyond the white lines on the outside of the corner. I always imagined there was a lovely, green meadow out there."

Today FIA and FIM safety inspectors often visit circuits together, each taking into consideration the other's concerns but, at the end of the day, the motorcycle GP inspector knows that the needs of riders and drivers, although similar, are not the same. Then he stands at the apex of the bend and looks toward the exit and then starts to pace off the metres, just like Franco Uncini did that winter day at 'the Kink'.

TELEVISION

Manel Arroyo took over Dorna's television department just prior to the start of the 1994 season. At that time the television package for broadcasters included all races and all classes, but there was still no uniformity in TV production. Dorna handled rights and distribution, rented satellites, supplied the uplink, organized the TV compound and, after the race, post-produced a highlights programme from the material that the host broadcaster provided, but had very little hand in the production of the signal.

Manel remembers not just the late nights as the Dorna team put out news access highlights, but also the long days of editing after the event. When races were back to back, editing crews barely had time to finish one Grand Prix before flying away to the next one.

"In those analogue times we had to edit mountains of BetaCam tape, voice it and send it," recalls Manel. "Our programme was called 'the Dorna 55' and we didn't get it out until Tuesday or Wednesday. In the early days, in order to edit in any shot from the beginning of the programme we had to wait until the end of the entire programme. Now, with digital, we can start our post-race highlights programme on Thursday before the race with a pre-race sound-bite from an interview and drop that into the first minute. That means the job is done at six o'clock on Sunday afternoon instead of late Wednesday evening."

Back in those early days, there was no uniformity in production from one Grand Prix to another and often, in the midst of an exciting fight for the lead, the host broadcaster might cut to a rider from his country circulating alone and out of the points.

"From the very beginning," continues Manel, "I was concerned when I saw that the broadcasters, when they produced their own event, did whatever they felt like and many times this didn't coincide with the way we believed a Grand Prix should be presented and transmitted. I remember, for example, one of the established GP broadcasters used a different TV director for each of the three races. A different director of production for 125cc, 250cc and 500cc. There was no consistent line.

"At another circuit I urged the director to make use of the onboard cameras, which offered unique shots from our sport and had cost us a lot of money, but he told me that they always showed the same view. I told him he had thrown me for a loop with that reply. The shot might look the same, I said, but we were seeing a lot of different things in that shot!

"In Japan, we had terrible language problems. I remember the Japanese director shot the grid bike-by-bike, rider-by-rider, for the international feed. It was a very good job, with on-screen graphics, stats and riders' names, but then, when he connected for the domestic audience, he started all over again at the beginning and ran what the international audience had already seen.

"Because of incongruities like that, we started working on a general model that has brought us where we are today. My argument when I spoke to the broadcasters was to say, 'You are the host broadcaster once a year, but you are a broadcaster 17 times a year and you should be concerned that the signal you receive always has the same look and feel for your viewers and that the race is shown in the same way by a single team that produces all the Grands Prix.'

"It was daunting in the beginning to enter those big BBC production and editing trucks… the BBC practically invented TV production! When we were new to this sport and this paddock, I used to be almost overwhelmed when I entered the trucks of the BBC, France TV or ESPN, but I came to realize, as we gained experience, that we could actually do a better job than these big companies because we were thinking every day of the year about how to televise motorcycle racing.

"We were aware that we were seen as a group of Spanish outsiders entering into a world that had traditionally been dominated by the British, the Americans, and the French and, in motorsports anyway, the Italians. They didn't say it, but it was easy to perceive that they were thinking, 'These guys, this company, what do they think they can teach us?'

"At least that is what we felt and those kinds of thoughts make you believe that just doing a good job is not enough. I don't want to call it a complex, just an awareness that, because we were new and from a country not known for motorsports TV production, we had to tie a bow on what we did… had to do something exceptional to make our work shine.

"I saw some of that same spirit in Australia with the people from FOX and from Channel 9 and Channel 10. Because Australia is so far off the beaten track, I think the Australians feel, just as we do, that they need to do something extra, something unexpected to give an extra glow to what they produce. I remember the privilege of working with Brian Morelli, the brilliant Australian director and one of the very best in the world at televising sporting events."

Generally, when a TV motorsports producer is asked about the most vividly recalled incident of a season, it will not be the excellent shot of the last-lap overtake, or the super-slow-motion shot of a deteriorating rear tyre down the Mugello straight at 350km/h. It will be of one of the near disasters in the TV compound that, hopefully, went unseen and unperceived. Manel remembers several.

"Once, just before the start of the 500cc race at Jacarepaguá, Brazil, we suddenly lost power to the TV compound. That was back in 1995 and we were working out of freight containers like those used for carrying cargo in trucks and on ships. We had all our editing suites and production and satellite uplink facilities set up in big windowless shipping containers. When the power failed and we realized that we had lost our international signal, we were maybe three minutes from the start, certainly no more than five, and we had one of our technicians crawling around under a freight container trying to reconnect Jacarepaguá with the world audience. One of the connections had come out of the junction box. I was on the walkie-talkie telling race direction on the grid to be prepared to delay the start when, just in time, the power came back.

ABOVE **SKY TV presenters Guido Meda and Vera Spadini open the season under the floodlights in Qatar 2017.**

"The time I remember most was a few years ago at Indianapolis when something we never imagined possible happened. A pair of the circuit's generators, the best available, caught fire, burst into flame, with seven laps to go in the MotoGP race and suddenly we lost all our track cameras. We had to finish the race relying on the onboard cameras, the helicopter camera and the RF (wireless) cameras, and the funny part of that was that some of the commentators didn't notice the change."

I was in the commentary booth that day and I remember thinking that Sergi Sendra, director of TV production for Dorna Sports, was getting rather creative! When the broadcast was over I caught Sergi's eye as we passed in the TV compound and his eye roll was eloquent.

"We were lucky that time," adds Manel, "because we were in the United States and the voltage to the track cameras was 110V running off the circuit's generators, but we were running all the material we brought from Europe on 220V. That meant we didn't lose the international feed and we could patch together shots from onboard, helicopter and RF cameras so

viewers around the world saw Marc Márquez win, although not from the usual angles. When situations like that happen, we notice the composure of our team, their confidence in their ability to manage situations. But, if there is one thing we can truly be proud of in Dorna, it is that we have established a TV-Media working arrangement that is considered today to be one of the references in the industry. This in itself is our main challenge every day: to continue to maintain this position."

There are times when technology runs into conflict with the sport itself. As Manel has learned over the years, one treads lightly when entering the inner sanctum of a MotoGP factory team garage.

"Thanks to Jeremy Burgess," continues Manel, "I learned how a race engineer views any interference into his garage and his world. At the time of this incident Jeremy was Mick Doohan's crew chief. Doohan was the reigning champion and the dominant rider of the period, the star of the 500cc class. It was in 1996 and I had convinced Carmelo to increase the TV budget to allow us to go beyond the two or three on-bike cameras that we had then. We had managed to procure and prepare ten on-bike cameras and were ready to mount them on ten bikes. And I, with my ten cameras, happy and unsuspecting, thought that now we would always have the top riders in the points riding bikes equipped with onboard cameras for the entire season. Maybe we'd even have cameras on all the likely leaders in every race!

"But when we went to the Honda team garage to give them this good news, Jeremy Burgess said, 'Don't even think about it!'"

It is easy to imagine Burgess, the most successful crew chief of the modern era, taking one look at the 1.7kg of unwelcome weight and showing the TV technicians the way out of the HRC garage.

Most of Dorna's ten expensive cameras spent the season travelling around the world in crates, but Dorna was determined. By working closely with the manufacturers, Dorna was able to gain the cooperation of the factories and include the obligatory use of onboard cameras in the technical regulations.

Today the onboard equipment transmits not only images but also speed, bike position and other data that is translated into on-screen graphics. Fitting a camera to a big NASCAR vehicle or an F1 car is relatively easy compared to working within the confines of a Grand Prix motorcycle. To quote Manel, "In comparison to our task of fitting our onboard equipment to the tiny space on a GP motorcycle, fitting a camera on a racing car is like installing something in a palace."

Every miniaturized, lightweight piece of kit that a GP bike carries must be the minimum expression of that component and that includes the most sophisticated gyroscopic on-bike cameras.

The engineers fought against carrying the onboard cameras until they realized that they were, to use Manel's words, "an irreversible and chronic evil that they simply could not avoid".

Then, being engineers, they included the camera in the design of the bike. By the end of the nineties, a Grand Prix bike came out of the factory with an engine, a clutch, wheels, brakes, a fuel tank and a camera mount.

If the engineers thought Dorna would be satisfied with just onboards, they soon found that Dorna TV wanted more. When Dorna asked to be allowed to tap into the ECU (engine control unit) and display the RPM (revs per minute) on screen, this was denied.

Undissuaded, the TV engineers designed a software program that could, with an algorithm, determine RPM from sound and they began running RPM data on screen. After a couple of races, a technician from a factory team came to the Dorna offices in the TV compound and asked to see the data graph. He laid the data taken directly from the ECU over the sound-derived data and said two words — 'You win' — and left. After that the factory teams allowed Dorna to plug into the ECU for RPM data.

Now fans have, as additional on-screen data, accurate and timely information about tyre choice in the MotoGP class by way of automatic tyre detection technology. Michelin supply tyres that send a signal identifying the type of tyres that each bike is running, both front and rear, and this information is immediately available to teams as well as to TV broadcasters. The data passes from the tyre to the bike's ECU and on to the track-timing system, which reports via an updated version of the unified software… much easier than trying to detect a line of colour on the sidewall of a tyre spinning at race speed.

Dorna is now delivering multi-screen options to Pay-TV viewers and is beginning to make those pictures available to broadcasters so that the viewer at home can decide to watch the race as it is cut by the director or to see the race from any of several shots. The viewer becomes the director of a personalized production, seeing what is happening at any point on the track, onboard from any one of several bikes, or from the pits, or from the helicopter, and from different angles.

At the final race of the season in Valencia 2016, Pol Espargaró's Yamaha was fitted with a camera that allowed some viewers at home, wearing special goggles and via computer, to look around and see what Pol was seeing during the race from the cockpit of the bike.

"New technology offers the TV viewer access to

BELOW The tiny onboard cameras now provide unbelievable footage in live pictures that are shown to millions throughout the world.

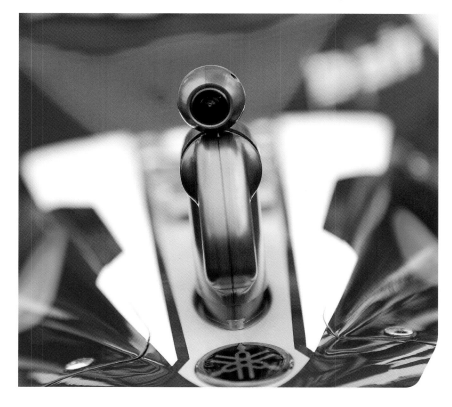

ABOVE Former 250cc World Champion and team owner Sito Pons was a big supporter of the switch to four-strokes.

experiences that are unique to our sport," concludes Manel. "Technology is evolving quickly and we are working with the highest quality equipment, ultra-high definition 4K… and we are going to offer to viewers the possibility of experiencing the race as our riders do, as if the viewer were at the controls of a MotoGP machine."

THE RETURN OF THE FOUR-STROKES

It was in the mid-nineties that former two-time 250cc World Champion Sito Pons, who was running a satellite Honda 500cc team, learned from discussions with Honda executives that the 500cc class was becoming irrelevant to the commercial interests of the Japanese manufacturers. Honda had decided to gradually stop building two-strokes altogether and, although the company remained committed to Grand Prix racing, Superbike racing was of more interest to their development engineers.

"The change to four-strokes was first suggested by Sito Pons," says Carmelo Ezpeleta. "In this Sito played a big part. He told me that the constructors wanted to change to four-strokes, engines related to the bikes they build for the street. I followed this up, talking first with Honda and Yamaha and then with the others, and, little by little, I began to form an idea. Ducati and Aprilia were interested but they believed that, given the level of the 500s, four-strokes would not be competitive. Honda, Yamaha and Suzuki were the only remaining manufacturers in 500 after Cagiva left. We kept talking and finally got around to the idea of giving the four-strokes a really big advantage… 1,000cc four-strokes against 500cc two-strokes. The idea was to move to only four strokes after a short transition period.

"The first year we had a mix of 990cc four-strokes and 500cc two-strokes — and the four-strokes won every race. Kawasaki joined Honda, Yamaha and Suzuki among the four-stroke entrants for 2002 and Aprilia was there too with their Cosworth engine. For 2003, the second year of the four-stroke regulations, Kenny Roberts, after entering the Modenas three-cylinder two-stroke in the opening rounds, turned to the five-cylinder 990cc Proton four-stroke to complete an all-four-stroke MotoGP grid that was joined that same year by Ducati with their V4 Desmosedici. It was a logical change, as was the change in the name of the class and the championship to MotoGP, but we moved slowly into the new era because not everyone supported such a big change at first."

To suggest a return to four-strokes to the 500cc class in the mid-to-late nineties seemed a crazy idea to many in a paddock that had not seen a four-stroke GP machine compete since the last race of the quixotic Honda NR500 in 1981. Few could remember 15-time World Champion Giacomo Agostini's *sayonara* win in the Nürburgring drizzle on the howling MV Agusta in 1976, the last GP win by a 500cc four-stroke. Kenny Roberts, who was often consulted by Carmelo, was one of the many who initially opposed the idea. He called the four-strokes "diesels" and said they would endanger riders due to oil leaks, but his opinions, based on his experiences in AMA races where two-strokes and four-strokes occasionally raced together, gradually changed.

"One thing I'm sure of," Kenny told me in a mid-nineties interview, "no matter what anybody says, whatever you spend on two-strokes, just double it, or maybe triple it, and that's what running a four-stroke will cost."

All the time the four-stroke concept was being discussed, timidly at first, Japanese manufacturers were more concerned with working to reduce contamination in advance of inevitable new emissions laws. The GP series was becoming technologically stagnant. Doohan's string of five world titles on the NSR500 was good for the brand but meant less to Honda's R&D Department than John Kocinski's SBK title on the RC45 in 1997. On the sporting side, racing was becoming too predictable and 500cc lap times and performance were not improving. For example, the lap record set at Assen by Kevin Schwantz in 1991 remained unbroken when the track configuration was altered for the 2002 season.

Valentino Rossi, motorcycle racing's most popular superstar, won the last 500cc title and the first MotoGP title, both on Hondas. Today, although many riders talk of the old days of the 500s, only Valentino, who recalls them with a combination of nostalgia, reverence and awe, speaks from experience.

The MotoGP four-stroke era began in 2002 with deafening cacophony: the familiar shriek of the 500s mixed with the bellow of the four-cylinder Yamaha and Suzuki four-strokes, the five-cylinder Hondas and Cosworth-powered three-cylinder Aprilias. A six-cylinder Blata never made it off the drawing board. What many of us thought was the sound of the high-revving four-strokes hitting the rev limiters was actually the stutter of the first traction-control systems. We all had a lot to learn.

I still remember the first time I saw a MotoGP rider come down through the gears for turn one at the Circuit of Catalunya without blipping the throttle. It seemed wrong. Four-strokes took GP racing into a new world of intrusive electronics. (Honda had only briefly experimented with fuel injection with the 500cc two-strokes in the nineties before turning back to carburation.) Early electronic engine management was more reactive than proactive and the adjustments to

prevent tyre spin on acceleration produced a riot of exhaust noise that, while understood by the technicians, sounded like either the activation of a rev limiter or a top-end misfire.

"One important element that we began to keep in mind as a vital part of the entertainment element of MotoGP," remembers Manel Arroyo, "was the sound of the engines. I still remember being with Carmelo in front of the Yamaha garage in order to listen, along with Yamaha's Lin Jarvis, to the Yamaha M1 as it passed down the straight. Carmelo had been reminding the manufacturers that sound was important. I remember Lin agreed. He said that it was not the sound we had been expecting."

Those long, open megaphones of the sixties and early seventies gave the exhaust noise of the four-stroke MV Agusta fours and triples and the four-cylinder Honda a thrilling howl, but the most powerful 990cc class four-strokes were producing close to 220bhp, about three times the output of the previous generation of Grand Prix four-strokes. Riders were dealing with wild wheel spinning on acceleration and wheel juddering and bouncing from engine braking on corner entry. Electronic rider aids on acceleration such as timing retardation or cutting one or two cylinders as a form of primitive traction control, or the use of 'throttle kickers' or even just a high idle on closed-throttle braking, gave the 990s a constantly evolving sound as technicians sought to smooth out the new engines. The old thunder of the three-into-three and four-into-four

FAR LEFT At the 1976 German Grand Prix at the old Nürburgring Giacomo Agostini was the last four-stroke winner until Valentino Rossi's success at Suzuka in 2002.

LEFT Such was the technical stagnation during the last decade of the 500cc two-strokes that Kevin Schwantz's 1991 lap record in the Dutch TT at Assen was not beaten until the circuit layout changed 11 years later.

ABOVE The last two-
stroke/four-stroke
showdown came at the
2002 German Grand Prix at
the Sachsenring when Alex
Barros and Olivier Jacque
led Valentino Rossi's four-
stroke Honda before they
crashed into each other,
handing Rossi victory.

500cc MV Agusta and Honda exhaust systems would
not return nor would the shriek of the five- and six-
pipe four-stroke Hondas in the smaller classes, but the
initial acoustic unpleasantness decreased as efficiency
was achieved and the 990s found their distinct and
incredibly loud 'voice'. Times were changing fast, and
lap times dropping. Aprilia's Cosworth engine, although
unsuccessful, brought automotive racing technology with
pneumatic valve closing and fly-by-wire throttle control,
but Honda initially used their classic sixties formula of
making more power with more cylinders and were
dominant with their five-cylinder engine at the beginning
of the new era, taking advantage of the fact that
four- and five-cylinder bikes were subject to the same
minimum weight.

By comparison, however, the previous 500cc two-
strokes had been much harder for riders to tame and for
technicians to manage. Wayne Rainey recalls the early
days of data acquisition in the late eighties and early
nineties. "Tom O'Kane was running sensors on our bike
and after practice we'd sit down and look at the data
collected… throttle opening on a 0-to-10 scale, RPM,
tyre temperatures, exhaust temperature, suspension

travel at different points… we didn't even have airboxes
until 1992 in Yamaha… and we'd sit down with all that
data and try and figure out what was going on and
how to make it better. Racing was changing and kept
changing when I was a team owner, but nothing like it
is today."

I remember walking up to the Team Roberts work
truck and being waved off by O'Kane, who said, "You
can't go in yet. The computer is still docking." Docking?
That was a mid-nineties glimpse of the 'big data' future.

But all that, the change from the days when, as a
journalist, I would occasionally walk into a garage and
see an engine, cases split and stripped down to a steel,
aluminium and 'unobtainium' jigsaw puzzle on the
bench, to today's NASA-like secrecy and tamper-proof
sealed engines, came slowly. When Dorna first came
into the series, some 125cc and 250cc riders still did
'plug chops' at the end of practice sessions and wise
old crew chiefs in the smaller classes still sniffed at
moisture in the air before deciding on jetting. Things
were already changing by the end of the eighties and
the beginning of the nineties. There were computers in
the factory work trucks and riders analysed data with

clean-handed crew members who had never been seen rebuilding a gearbox.

Eddie Lawson once told his crew chief, Erv Kanemoto, in 1989 that he was "flat out" through a particular corner but Kanemoto, data in hand, showed him that he was nowhere near full throttle. Eddie, it is told, looked at the data and said, "You know, I really hate that damn thing." The computer, "that damn thing", became prominent when MotoGP went to four-strokes in 2002. How different were those times? This different: I remember overhearing Freddie Spencer say to Kanamoto in 1985 as he parked the 250cc prior to going straight back out on the 500, "It feels lean but I think it still might be rich." And Erv nodded; two-stroke debrief concluded.

Wayne Rainey: "Kenny Roberts was always pushing to get more sensors on my bike, more data, and we got some pushback from Yamaha. 'What do you need all this stuff for?' they asked. Today's four-strokes probably record more data on a single lap than we'd log in a season!"

RULES OF THE ROAD

Prior to 1992, Grand Prix motorcycle events were largely under the control of national federation officials and alternating FIM stewards. One of the first major changes was to appoint a Permanent Race Director and Permanent Race Direction group. Over these past 25 years there have been four Race Directors: Pierpaolo Gardella, Roberto Nosetto, Paul Butler and, currently, Mike Webb. The job of Race Direction is, primarily,

enforcement of sporting rules and the running of the racing programme from the tower, but rule-making takes place in quieter rooms.

Compared to other forms of motorsport, changes to sporting and technical regulations in Grand Prix motorcycle racing were relatively few during the 20th century. A 50cc class was added in 1962 and then changed to 80cc in 1984. There was a major overhaul of technical regulations at the beginning of the seventies and then, in the eighties, two of the racing classes were eliminated: the 350cc class after 1982 and the 80cc class after 1989. Sidecar racing left the GP paddock during the nineties but continues under FIM sanction. Other significant and relatively recent rule changes were the switch from push starts to engine-running starts in 1987 and the banning of leaded fuel in 1998, but the move to four-strokes in MotoGP, Moto2 and finally Moto3 meant a major rewrite and fattening of the FIM Grand Prix rule book.

There have been more significant rule changes since the first race of the MotoGP class in 2002 until the present than in the previous 53 years. Understanding how the championship got from where it was at the end of the 500cc era to where it is today requires looking at how and why some of the most important rules were made.

The greatest responsibility of the MotoGP championship organizers and rule-makers, after safety, is to find a suitable compromise between technological evolution, affordable racing and that most vital element

LEFT In 2016, the climax year of the 25-year revolution, Michelin became sole tyre supplier in MotoGP.

often referred to disparagingly as 'the show'. The rule-making process in MotoGP today rests with the four members of the Grand Prix Commission. IRTA is directly concerned with sporting regulations and the MSMA with technical regulations. The FIM is the sanctioning body while Dorna is directly involved in all aspects, sporting, technical, commercial and those regarding safety. Dorna is represented by Carmelo Ezpeleta who also chairs the Commission. The FIM is represented by Paul Duparc (previously by Claude Danis and Ignacio Verneda), IRTA is represented by Hervé Poncharal and the MSMA by Takanao Tsubouchi. Mike Trimby acts as secretary, a position previously held by Paul Butler.

The ultimate authority over MotoGP resides with the Permanent Bureau. Rules proposed to the Grand Prix Commission are, if approved, submitted to the two-member Permanent Bureau for ratification or veto by current FIM President Vito Ippolito and Carmelo Ezpeleta.

When Dorna first acquired FIM rights, the championship was composed of three classes that no longer exist today. The 125cc, 250cc and 500cc classes are equated, both in the record books and in the minds of fans, with the current Moto3, Moto2 and MotoGP categories, but today's bikes have little in common with the machines they replaced. No change, however, was ever so impactful for Grand Prix fans, teams and riders as the morphing of the 500cc class into MotoGP in 2002, and then, after two years, the final disappearance of the 500cc two-strokes. This was followed by the replacement of the 250cc class by Moto2

in 2010 and of the 125cc class by Moto3 in 2012.

The MotoGP class has gone through many rule changes since its inception. There was a weight-to-number-of-cylinders formula for the 990s from 2002 to 2006. From 2007 to 2011 the 800cc machines were limited to four cylinders and that limit continues at the time of writing with the 1,000cc bikes. The number of engines per rider for the season was set with a formula based on prior results. More fuel and more engines were allowed for new manufacturers and for manufacturers whose riders had *not* achieved a set minimum number of wins and/or podiums the previous season or during the season in progress. Fuel limits, originally 24 litres, went down to 22, to 20 and then back to 22 when the standard ECU was approved for the 2016 season. Tyres were limited first by number per race and per rider, and then, for the first time in the premier class, a single tyre supplier was appointed for the 2009 season. During the 2017 season, each class had an assigned exclusive tyre supplier: Dunlop in Moto3 and Moto2, and Michelin (replacing Bridgestone at the beginning of 2016) in MotoGP.

Technical rule changes during the MotoGP era were almost always agreed upon or rejected unanimously by the MSMA, but in the case of the obligatory ECU imposed from 2016 the members of the manufacturers' association were unable to agree. This rare lack of unanimity allowed the measure, supported by the FIM, Dorna and IRTA, to pass without full support from the manufacturers.

BELOW Dorna's adoption of four-stroke combustion became complete in 2012 when the old 125cc category was replaced by Moto3, for single-cylinder 250cc machinery.

THE CRT GAMBIT: MISSION ACCOMPLISHED

Although often ignored in analyses of MotoGP history, the brief but significant existence of the CRT (Claiming Rules Teams) class deserves attention. The MotoGP class began in 2002 with a grid of 21 machines, a mixture of four-stroke 990cc machines and two-stroke 500cc ones. While attention was centred on the battles at the front, the grid grew from an average of 20.6 machines in 2002 to 23.25 in 2003 and an almost identical average in 2004. Then the tide began gradually to turn. The racing at the front was thrilling with factory machines breaking lap records, but over the combined 2010 and 2011 seasons the average grid size slipped to 16.4 machines and the sight of only 14 bikes under starter's orders at Phillip Island in 2011 marked a low point that had not been reached since only 13 500s started the 1991 Austrian Grand Prix. Something had to be done, but the manufacturers, then engaged in replacing the 800cc bikes with a new generation of 1,000cc bikes, were unable, they said, to offer 'satellite-spec' racing bikes to independent teams at affordable prices.

Dorna reacted by creating the CRT class, allowing the use of production-derived engines. The origin of the name 'Claiming Rules Teams' lay in the fact that, to hold down costs and to avoid factories providing special components to select non-factory teams, CRT machines could be 'claimed' and purchased by other factory teams at a set cost. No machine was ever claimed but the rule prevented the possibility of 'satellite-spec' bikes being entered in the Open class.

The CRTs, with their 'hot-rod' street engines, were slower but, although maligned in the specialist press for their performance, the class did its job of bringing the MotoGP grid back to an average of 20.7 in 2012 and up to just under 24 bikes per race in 2013. The brief CRT episode showed manufacturers that, if they did not find a way to increase the number of competitive MotoGP machines, there was an alternative.

The MSMA now understood the problem and a new designation of racing machine was devised: Open bikes. Honda and Ducati offered Open versions of factory bikes with less sophistication and performance than their factory and satellite bikes. (Yamaha initially leased engines to independent CRT teams that supplied their own chassis.) These Open class bikes, introduced

ABOVE The old two-stroke 250cc class made way in 2010 for Moto2, in which bikes use a four-stroke 600cc Honda engine.

in 2014, were limited to standard Magneti Marelli electronics but allowed 24 litres of fuel and 12 engines per rider per season compared to five engines per rider per season and 20 litres of fuel for teams designated as Factory Option. Special soft-compound tyres were available to Open bikes but the hard compound was denied them under the assumption that they did not have enough power to work the hard option tyres up to race temperature. A third category of machines called 'Factory Option with Concessions' began the season under Open rules but the riders of these bikes lost use of the soft tyres and their fuel load was reduced to 22 litres of fuel if certain results criteria were achieved. It was all very complicated for journalists, commentators and fans, but it was, in fact, a preparation for the future. At the time of writing manufacturers that are new to the MotoGP class or manufacturers that have not won a race in dry conditions since 2013 are allowed two more engines (nine instead of seven) than the basic rules permit. These manufacturers are also allowed unlimited testing and are able to continue engine development during the season.

The return of Suzuki in 2015, of Aprilia in 2016 and the arrival of KTM in 2017, each with two-rider factory teams, bolstered the field as they joined Ducati, fielding eight machines, Honda, with five entries, and Yamaha with four.

A standard Magneti Marelli ECU was mandated in 2015 for all machines except those classified as Factory Option and this unit became the basis of the obligatory ECU for the entire class as of 2016. (See Kevin Cameron's chapter on technical evolution).

The introduction of this standard ECU was one of the most contested issues to arise in the past 25 years. To factory riders in 2016, it felt initially like a step back to the days of the first 990s, but it is now an accepted part of the rules package. The CRT class served its purpose well and was extinct by 2014, but the Open class of machines that followed was an important step in controlling costs and increasing the universe of competitive MotoGP bikes as evidenced by full grids of competitive bikes and by the record nine winners in the 2016 season.

FLAG TO FLAG AND 'AERO BODY' RULES

One of the most difficult and delicate problems that the Grand Prix Commission has had to deal with concerns a problem unique to motorcycle racing: what to do about dry races that turn wet. A satisfactory set of rules for stopping and restarting the Moto3 and Moto2 races was found. Races in those classes that begin in the dry and then are stopped due to rain are restarted as a new race over a distance that, combined with laps completed before the red flag, completes the required minimum distance. But all members of the Grand Prix Commission agreed that the premier MotoGP class should complete full race distance whenever possible.

After many ideas were discussed and some tried, Dorna suggested taking advantage of the fact that MotoGP teams are allowed two machines and simply have the riders come in when authorized to do so by Race Direction and change to bikes fitted with tyres appropriate for the conditions. The 'flag to flag' rule, as it is called, was approved over initial objections from the majority of the MSMA members. Most traditionalists in the MotoGP paddock thought 'flag to flag' was a bad idea. In practice, however, it has worked well and become such a part of MotoGP racing that it is hard to imagine a better solution.

"The change to 'flag to flag'," explains Manel Arroyo, "was the solution to a major problem, a solution that worked for the FIM, the teams, the factories and also for Dorna TV. We once had a race, the Grand Prix of Catalunya in 2000, which, because of rain and restarts, ended at 5:30 in the afternoon. How many broadcasters stayed until the end? Very few. Most TV stations had commitments to other programming and they cut away. That race caused us to start talks and negotiations with the teams, the sponsors and, most of all, the riders themselves. There is a lot of competition for that 2:00pm Sunday time slot and, thanks to 'flag to flag', the Grand Prix Commission found a way to avoid delays without compromising safety."

BELOW In both years of the brief CRT era, 2012 and 2013, Aleix Espargaró was the highest-placed rider in the MotoGP points standings, racing an ART for the Aspar team of Jorge Martínez.

Another safety problem arose when the change from 800cc to 1,000cc gave riders a big boost in power and torque and that brought a wheelie problem. Initially electronic rider aids served to keep the front down during acceleration off corners but the manufacturers, anticipating the 2016 limits on electronics, were already experimenting with aerodynamic winglets in 2015. When the new limits on electronics were applied in 2016, winglets became commonplace. While technicians were at work testing different configurations for different circuits, riders went to the Safety Commission with concerns about the possibility of injuries from contact between a rider and a winglet. Some riders reported violent downstream turbulence when slipstreaming a bike equipped with winglets. These safety considerations led to the external winglets being banned for 2017 but aerodynamic development quickly turned to fairing design with a variety of 'gills' and scoops enclosing winglets to produce downforce. New 'Aero Body' rules adopted by the Grand Prix Commission will govern this evolving technology and require interpretation and enforcement by the FIM Technical Director and the Grand Prix Commission.

(Current FIM Technical Director is Danny Aldridge, who replaced Mike Webb when Webb became Permanent Race Director. The first FIM Technical Director was the late Jack Findlay, a Grand Prix winner and former FIM Formula 750 Champion.)

Mike Trimby believes the original philosophy of the four-member Grand Prix Commission that continues to this day has made problem-solving much easier and more satisfactory to all parties. "I know that F1 teams look at our rule-making structure and how it has continued to work for 25 years and they feel a certain degree of envy."

"WE SOUGHT STABILITY"

Carmelo Ezpeleta: "The idea was to listen to the manufacturers because they are the ones who build the bikes. We sought stability, so having rules packages in place for five years was a good start.

"We began with 990cc four-strokes and no limit on the number of cylinders and no maximum bore size. After the first five years, the MSMA wanted to go to 800cc because it was more of a technical challenge, but we soon saw that these engines were

ABOVE High-jump champion Marc Márquez shows perfect flag-to-flag technique.

too dependent on electronics so, five years later, we decided to return to 1,000cc, but we set an 81mm maximum piston diameter, more or less in line with the most extreme street-bike engines. This opened the door to smaller teams, allowing them to power their bike with a modified production engine. We called them CRTs. The CRTs were an intermediate step so that the manufacturers would see that we were capable of filling out the grid with bikes that they did not directly supply… the CRTs weren't as good as factory satellite bikes, but they allowed private teams to race and have a healthy bottom line.

"When the factories finally understood that we needed full grids, not just a few factory bikes, and understood that we would do whatever was necessary provide full grids, they changed their policy and started offering Open bikes to private teams. Honda offered complete bikes and Yamaha leased engines. Ducati are leasing Open bikes too and eventually all the participating factories will as well. With Moto2 and Moto3 the problem was not the number of bikes but the lack of manufacturers. It was not my idea to propose a single-brand series, but it was the only way and we are happy with the outcome.

"When we introduced Moto2 in 2010, the World Superbike promoter tried to stop us from using a 600cc production engine until the FIM ruled that we could use production engines as long as there was no model of street bike that was marketed to the public as a Moto2 racer. To the Moto3 class, introduced in 2012, we

applied the same maximum piston diameter of 81mm, but with an RPM limit to keep costs down. The current Moto3 250cc engine formula is basically one cylinder of a four-cylinder MotoGP engine and with a rev limit to control costs.

"Returning to MotoGP, when we changed back from 800cc to 1,000cc, we also decided to introduce a standard ECU to lower costs and to help satellite teams be competitive. This was a battle because the factories were against it. In one case, a manufacturer said that if we imposed a generic ECU they would quit MotoGP and go to Superbikes, but that statement was made without the manufacturer knowing that two months before Superbikes had come under Dorna's management. I understand why the manufacturers resisted. But I think now they understand why we had to have a standard ECU and why, from time to time, regulations must change."

I asked Carmelo to what extent he thought that the fact that MotoGP produced a record number of nine winners during the 2016 season could be attributed to the standard ECU.

"I think the ECU rule is part of the cause, but it's also because of the depth of the field. The level of talent over the entire grid has never been higher. From the beginning we have worked to encourage and develop young riders, first in the Spanish CEV, the FIM CEV (now the Junior World Championship) and also in the Asia Talent Cup. Alberto Puig has worked hard to develop young riders for us and continues to do so. But talent

BELOW This is the 50th anniversary tribute to the great Ángel Nieto, at Assen in 2016. The prominent people are (from left) Álex Crivillé, Carmelo Ezpeleta, Gelete Nieto, Ángel Nieto, Pablo Nieto, Mike Trimby and Jorge 'Áspar' Martínez. Ángel Nieto passed away in August 2017.

ABOVE Dorna started with a dozen personnel in 1992 – what a contrast in this team photograph at Valencia in 2016.

needs opportunity. Moto3 and Moto2 offer a path. Now we have four factories winning races in MotoGP and Aprilia is working and KTM is joining too. We are also seeing that Superbike, both at world and national level, may offer an alternative path. We are helping MotoAmerica as well. I think the steps we have taken with rules have been well thought out and correct.

"The truth is that it has taken us longer to get where we wanted to go than we originally thought, but I have always been obsessed with trying to convince rather than imposing our will. We could have made the changes before we did in some cases because, with the FIM and IRTA supporting us, we could have out-voted the MSMA 3-1, but instead we worked to convince the MSMA of the merit of our ideas."

This final portion of this piece is based on an interview in Carmelo's paddock office in Valencia on the Wednesday before the final race of the 2016 season. We had been talking for an hour and we both realized the we could have talked for hours more, just as I realized when I sat down to write this text that the full version of these past 25 years could fill a book twice this size and leave little room for pictures. Somewhere

during our conversation that day in Valencia the phrase "the secret to success" arose. Carmelo picked up on that and said, "You know, I think we have covered practically everything, much more than you'll be able to fit in the book, but I just remembered something… I remember the day Steve McLaughlin came to sell me a million-dollar secret… in fact it was you who said he wanted to sell me a big secret… he came to Madrid to that office I had over on Calle Hernández de Tejada, the place where I had a single office in the entire building and there was a dog that was always running up and down barking all day long. Steve, a true original, came in with his white straw hat and his secret. He wanted me to pay up front and I said no. I said, 'First you tell me the secret and if I apply it, I will pay you.' And he said that to find out I had to pay first. That was 25 years ago. And we left it that way, he without the million and I without the secret. Maybe the secret was under his hat. We still laugh about that whenever we meet."

And we both laughed. That, the laughter, is a big part of what I remember of those 25 years. May the next 25 years be just as exciting and just as much fun.

PART 2

THE RACING ERAS

THE WORLD CHAMPIONSHIP STORY

Governor's Bridge on the Isle of Man TT mountain course
— where the World Championship was born in 1949.

CHAPTER 4

1949–1991
BIRTH OF A DREAM

BY JUAN PEDRO DE LA TORRE

It would be impossible to write about the World Championship of motorcycle racing without taking a look at the pre-history of this sport. In its early inception, motorcycle racing was connected with two names that are synonyms with competitive racing: the Grand Prix and the Continental Circus.

The first use of the name Grand Prix for a motorcycle race was in 1904, for the Paris Coupe Internationale des Motocyclettes, with riders from France, Denmark, Germany, Britain and Austria. The Fédération Internationale des Clubs Motocyclistes (FICM) was founded the following day and this organization regulated European racing competitions for over 40 years.

RIGHT The second round of the inaugural World Championship in 1949 was a combined car and motorcycle meeting at Berne in Switzerland.

Racing was born and developed hand-in-hand with the motorcycle manufacturing industry, growing and evolving with it. In this discipline, there always was and always will be a close relationship between manufacturing and sport. Competitive racing found fertile ground in nations with a booming motorcycle industry such as Britain, Germany and Italy, countries that became the undisputed leaders in motorcycle racing, in terms of both competition and technology.

Although there were many different races in Europe and the United States, some became so prominent and prestigious that they attracted riders from other countries. Once the main competitions were consolidated, racers criss-crossed the Old Continent to compete. Riders eventually formed groups and toured as a collective, not unlike a circus troupe. Hence the name Continental Circus, for the cyclical tour that began every spring.

THE EUROPEAN GRAND PRIX

The inter-war period (1919–1939) was particularly prosperous for all areas of motorsport and booming interest in motorcycle racing motivated the FICM to launch its first official championship: the European Grand Prix. Every year, races in several countries shared the common name 'Grand Prix', but the FICM decided to create an official title to add importance to the contests.

The European Grand Prix was a title bestowed to an individual Grand Prix, rotating each year, and was held from 1924 to 1937. The first two editions took place at Monza, which was inaugurated in 1922 and was regarded as the most advanced race track of its time. After 1938, the European Grand Prix became the European Championship, which included several races and three distinct, more tightly regulated competitive classes: 250cc, 350cc and 500cc. Up to that point, the European Grand Prix had included a wide range of

categories from 125cc to 1,000cc and even three classes of sidecars.

After the Second World War, competition resumed in 1947 in the same spirit as in 1924, with a single race, but under the new name of the 'European Championship'. However, the new competition had only two editions. At the end of 1948 the FICM decided to replace it the following year with a World Championship.

THE WORLD CHAMPIONSHIP

The idea of a motorcycle racing World Championship was received with great enthusiasm. The official rules were written in January 1949 and a six-race calendar was published the following month. The races were the Isle of Man Tourist Trophy (TT), the Grand Prix of Switzerland, the Dutch TT, the Belgian Grand Prix, the Ulster Grand Prix and the Nations Grand Prix in Italy. The competition was established as a championship for riders and manufacturers with five categories: 125cc, 250cc, 350cc, 500cc and 600cc sidecars.

This was the first time the Isle of Man Tourist Trophy was included in a Grand Prix. Until that time it had been

ABOVE On 13 June 1949 Freddie Frith takes the chequered flag at the 350cc TT race on the Isle of Man to become the first-ever winner of a World Championship race.

LEFT British rider Les Graham won that first 1949 500cc World Championship for the AJS factory.

ABOVE Bruno Ruffo leads Dario Ambrosini at the start of the 1951 250cc race at Berne in Switzerland. They went on to finish first and second in that first 250cc World Championship.

RIGHT The 1950 Dutch TT programme. Assen is the only circuit to have remained on the World Championship calendar from the start.

considered the 'race of races' and was held separately from the rest of European competitions. The TT had never held a championship race, either as part of the European Grand Prix or the European Championship. After the war, the connection between Britain and Europe seemed stronger, so perhaps it no longer made sense for the country to remain outside the World Championship. And, which other race could occupy that spot if not the Tourist Trophy?

The first edition introduced a qualifying system that was slightly modified in 1950. Originally, the classification was based on a net points system, calculated as a sum of individual results, plus an extra point for the fastest lap. As not all categories had the same number of races, a very simple formula was introduced in 1950 — and remained in use until 1975 — to calculate the number of races for each category. If the number of championship rounds was even, it was divided by two, plus one. The final number was the number of the best race results to be counted. If the number of races was odd, the calculation was based on the number of races, plus one, divided by two. In 1976 the championship was split into two tiers of five races each, with the three best results counting from each tier. From 1977 every result counted for the final standings, except in 1991, when the two worst results were deducted.

By the end of 1949, the FICM modified its statutes and changed its name to the Fédération Internationale de Motocyclisme (FIM).

From the beginning of the World Championship, Italy and Britain were dominant. After Germany was readmitted into the FIM in 1950, German riders and manufacturers began competing that year. However, an alliance between the French and the British introduced a ban on the use of superchargers, an advantage that had allowed German manufacturers BMW and DKW to surpass rivals in the 1930s.

The World Championship was something of a stalemate during its first years. Italian riders and manufacturers ruled in 125cc and 250cc, while the British were undisputed kings in the bigger categories, although that did not last for long. Italian industry kept growing in volume and the number of manufacturers, producing lots of new brands that slowly reduced the British advantage. The remaining British factories — AJS in 500cc, Velocette in 350cc, and Norton — were swallowed by an avalanche of Italian manufacturers: Moto Guzzi, Gilera, Mondial, MV Agusta, Morini and Benelli. The German NSU grew strong between 1952 and 1956 but then quickly faded.

Legendary names emerged in those initial years. Riders were grown men of great courage who became

ABOVE Nello Pagani, seen at Assen in 1949, was crowned the first 125cc World Champion at the end of that season.

LEFT What a line-up: Gilera prepares for the 1953 season. The riders are (from left) Geoff Duke, Giuseppe Colnago, Alfredo Milani and Umberto Masetti.

ABOVE Geoff Duke, with the Lancashire red rose proudly emblazoned on his helmet, won the third of his 500cc world titles riding the Gilera in 1954.

RIGHT The legendary Spa-Francorchamps road course hosted the World Championship from the start and the last Belgian Grand Prix was held there in 1990.

heroes on the race track. One such was Leslie Graham, a war-time RAF pilot who became the first World Champion in 500cc. The first decade of the World Championship saw the rise of other greats such as Carlo Ubbiali, a great champion in 125cc and 250cc; Geoff Duke, the first great king of 500cc; and John Surtees, the only rider in history to win the World Championship in 500cc and Formula One.

COMINGS AND GOINGS

The history of the World Championship is marked by the comings and goings of some of its main protagonists. In 1957 the final round of the World Championship was the Nations Grand Prix at Monza, where the undisputed superiority of Italian manufacturers was clearly evident, but a few weeks later Moto Guzzi, Gilera and Mondial all announced their withdrawal from racing in a mutual decision known as the 'Abstention Pact', citing rising costs and declining sales. MV Agusta, however, did not pull out and Count Agusta's team found itself in total command of the next three seasons: they won every rider and manufacturer title in all four motorcycle categories,

ABOVE John Surtees in action on the MV Agusta in 1956. He took his first world title that year and went on to win seven in all before switching to four wheels and finding success there too.

LEFT Carlo Ubbiali won the 125cc World Championship five times for MV Agusta after taking his first title in 1951 riding the Mondial.

and 80 per cent of all races. Never again would a single manufacturer win on such a scale.

That streak was too grand to sustain, even for MV Agusta, an aviation manufacturer with a small motorcycle division. The situation called for a counterbalance, which arrived in 1959 with a new and unexpected contestant — Honda.

Honda made its début in the TT of 1959 and undertook its first full season in 1960, in 125cc and 250cc, categories from which MV Agusta withdrew to focus on the biggest classes, although its participation in 1961 was in an unofficial capacity as the Italian company loaned its motorcycles to the Rhodesian rider, Gary Hocking, who won that year's 350cc and 500cc titles.

The void left by the Italian firms helped Honda to grow, along with other smaller manufacturers such as MZ of East Germany. Propelled by the talent of its engineer, Walter Kaaden, MZ had a winning streak with its two-stroke engine but that was undermined when its star rider, Ernst Degner, defected to the west, taking MZ's technical secrets with him. Degner's escape opened the way for Suzuki to become the second Japanese participant in the World Championship.

ABOVE Honda arrived on the Isle of Man from Japan in 1959 with four 125cc machines for the TT races — and the rest is history.

BELOW Australian Tom Phillis brought Honda its first World Championship success by winning the 1961 125cc title with four Grand Prix victories.

LEFT In 1963 New Zealander Hugh Anderson gave Suzuki two World Championship titles, in 50cc (pictured) and 125cc.

LEFT Seven-times World Champion Phil Read brought Yamaha four 250cc titles, starting in 1964.

THE GOLDEN AGE

The sixties were marked by the domination of Japanese manufacturers. The first two, Honda and Suzuki, were joined in 1963 by Yamaha, and later Kawasaki — more discreetly — took part too.

The sixties also opened up the World Championship to new venues outside Europe. Although the number of participants had grown in the years up to and including 1960, all the races had been held in Europe, but in 1961 the Grand Prix contenders travelled to Argentina and in 1963 to Japan, which, of course, was the logical consequence of the growing influence of the Japanese factories in motorcycle racing.

Another change was the introduction in 1962 of a new category, 50cc, which allowed the participation of new European manufacturers such as Derbi and Kreidler. However, these newcomers also had to measure themselves against the Japanese, who quickly moved into all categories.

Using different strategies, Honda, Suzuki and Yamaha all became World Champions in the sixties. Between 1961 and 1968, Japanese manufacturers achieved 30 constructors' titles and 30 riders' titles. Only in the 500cc class did Europeans manage to maintain their supremacy, largely thanks to the strength of MV Agusta, which was challenged only by Honda. It was in the 500cc category that two of the greatest figures in motorcycle racing history measured up against each other in a legendary duel: Mike Hailwood and Giacomo Agostini.

This was an age of incredible technical advancement. Japanese manufacturers showed unbridled growth, producing a series of exceptional new models. But progress was as fleeting as it was fast. The FIM soon announced regulatory changes, introducing new rules for the 50cc class in 1967, and changes for the other categories in 1968. Honda swiftly announced its withdrawal from the championship and, a few months later, Yamaha and Suzuki also stated that they would pull out at the end of 1968.

At the time the general belief was that the Japanese exodus was caused by the regulation changes, which prevented factories from developing multi-cylinder machinery and forced them instead to produce completely new models for virtually every category by 1970. However, the real reason was the state of the Japanese economy and, in particular, over-production, a phenomenon that took Japan to the verge of a huge crisis.

Without Japanese participation, the World Championship became the domain of small 'artisanal' manufacturers, with the sole exception of MV Agusta, which maintained its tight grip on the 350cc and 500cc categories.

ABOVE Pin-up boy — Giacomo Agostini was a massive star both on and off the track.

LEFT The sound of the sixties — this is 1968 and Mike Hailwood's Honda leads the MV Agusta of Giacomo Agostini in a non-championship race at Rimini.

ABOVE Grand Prix racing lost one of its greatest when Jarno Saarinen was killed in 1973 at Monza in Italy.

MISTROVSTVÍ SVĚTA
GRAND PRIX ČSSR
BRNO
22. 8. 1976
PROGRAM Kčs 5,-

RIGHT The Grand Prix at Brno in the Czech Republic (formerly Czechoslovakia) joined the World Championship calendar in 1965 and has remained a riders' favourite ever since.

MODERN TIMES

The seventies brought about important changes. The first was the technological revolution based on the rise of the two-stroke engine. This configuration was already popular in the small and medium categories, but it eventually conquered 500cc too, marking the end of MV Agusta's reign.

The Italian manufacturer had ruled undisputed in 500cc from 1958 to 1974, but the roaring two-strokes outpaced its four-stroke engines. The demise of MV Agusta also coincided with the retirement of Giacomo Agostini, whose last title came in 1975, with Yamaha in 500cc. Nobody has ever matched the Italian's record of 15 World Championships and 122 Grand Prix victories.

The sweeping regulation changes imposed early in this decade put a serious technical limitation on machinery and were prompted by concern that a rapid rise in costs, resulting from the development of exotic multi-cylinder engines, might put some factories in financial peril. The new rules meant that 50cc machines were restricted to single-cylinder engines from 1969, and the following season all 125cc and 250cc bikes were limited to two cylinders. And from 1974 in the

elite 500cc class engines could not have more than four cylinders and six-speed gearboxes had to be used.

Yamaha's exile lasted only until 1973, when it returned to Grand Prix racing with the first-generation YZR500 and YZR250 machines. As well as unveiling a range of new machinery, Yamaha began working with a new star in the form of Finnish flyer Jarno Saarinen.

Saarinen won the 1972 250cc title and at the beginning of 1973 enjoyed instant success with Yamaha, doubling up with victories in the 250cc and 500cc races in the first two rounds, in France and Australia. Tragedy struck, however, in the fourth round, at Monza, when Saarinen was killed in the 250cc race in an incident that also claimed the life of Renzo Pasolini.

Yamaha immediately halted its factory racing activities in Grand Prix racing for the rest of the year and only returned in 1974, with Agostini taking Saarinen's place.

When Suzuki decided to return to the fold, it only had one area of focus and that was to dominate the 500cc class with the superb RG500. Suzuki made good on its promise to take over the premier class

ABOVE Giacomo Agostini switched to Yamaha and in 1975 brought the company its first 500cc world title — and the first in the premier class for a two-stroke machine.

LEFT The 1979 Belgian Grand Prix programme — two years earlier Barry Sheene averaged 217.370km/h to win the race at Spa-Francorchamps.

ABOVE King Kenny Roberts arrived from America in 1978 and totally changed the face of Grand Prix motorcycle racing while winning three 500cc titles.

when it won seven manufacturers' titles in a row between 1976 and 1982 and took individual glory with Barry Sheene, Marco Lucchinelli and Franco Uncini.

Yamaha and Suzuki had marked the way forward with their two-stroke mastery and this engine configuration would take over all categories of the World Championship.

The second area of change in the seventies was safety, marked by the gradual phasing out of road racing in favour of racing on permanent tracks. Unfortunately, tragedy persisted, but riders no longer accepted it as inevitable, and on many occasions faced up to championship organizers to demand better safety measures. Their refusal to participate at dangerous circuits resulted in a massive boycott against the TT, which departed from the World Championship in 1977.

The decade also saw the 'professionalization' of motorcycle racing, with the introduction of sports marketing and advertising. This propelled the World Championship to a whole new level. American riders arrived, led by Kenny Roberts, who not only popularized a new racing style but also a new attitude beyond the race track.

New financial factors, such as television rights, also played a role. Clashing interests and discontent resulted in huge conflict in the FIM. The World Series, an alternative championship led by Roberts, was motivated by safety concerns but ultimately failed.

The eighties saw further transformations. The 350cc category was phased out in 1983, and in the following year 50cc became the new 80cc class. New regulations introduced in 1988 limited 125cc engines to having only one cylinder, bringing it closer to the 80cc category and ultimately killing it, the 80cc category having its last season in 1989.

Another legend retired in the eighties: Ángel Nieto, 13-times World Champion in 50cc and 125cc. He retired after the 1986 season but his contribution to the World Championship in Spain and the role he played in the history of Dorna can never be underestimated.

Long before Álex Crivillé, Jorge Lorenzo and Marc Márquez became modern-day heroes to Spain's devoted motorcycling fans, Nieto was his nation's first two-wheeled superstar. Confident, charismatic and deeply superstitious, Nieto became a national hero and household name in his native Spain in an illustrious

World Championship career that spanned more than two decades.

Only Giacomo Agostini and Valentino Rossi have won more World Championship races than Nieto, who became the undisputed master of the lightweight 50cc, 80cc and 125cc categories. He won a total of 90 races and became a World Champion in the 50cc class six times and in the 125cc division an incredible seven times. Being a superstitious character, though, Nieto always referred to his 13 titles as '12+1'.

Nieto's journey to stardom started to take off when he took his first win, at Germany's Sachsenring 50cc race in 1969. Later that same season he collected his first World Championship title for Derbi when he defeated Dutch rider Aalt Toersen by a single point.

More success followed for Nieto and Derbi before he won the 1975 50cc title for Kreidler. He then took the 1976 and 1977 50cc crowns for Bultaco before further success followed on board Minarelli machinery in the 125cc class in 1979 and 1981. The Nieto love affair with winning did not stop there and his last three World Championship successes came for Garelli between 1982 and 1984.

Nieto is also notable for his unique achievement of being the only rider in Grand Prix history to win world titles for five different manufacturers, including the legendary Derbi brand, which he helped transform into one of the most recognisable and distinguished names in World Championship history.

It was perhaps fitting that Nieto's final Grand Prix

victory came riding for the legendary Derbi marque again in the 80cc class in 1985. He was facing his first winless season since 1973 when Derbi drafted him into its 80cc camp to support Jorge Martínez 'Áspar' in the French round at Le Mans. Martínez was trailing Swiss rider Stefan Dorflinger in the rankings

LEFT There has been a World Championship Grand Prix in Argentina sporadically since 1961 and in 1982 it was the scene of Honda's return to the 500cc battleground.

BELOW Before he became so involved in modern-day rider safety, Franco Uncini won the 1982 500cc world title for Suzuki.

ABOVE The late, great Ángel Nieto won one of his 13 World Championship titles in 1975 riding the 50cc Kreidler.

RIGHT History was made in 1983 when Grand Prix motorcycle racing was held on the African continent for the first time, at Kyalami in South Africa.

but the Spaniard's bike failed to start. Nieto, released from his role as support act, rolled back the years with a vintage display of riding to defeat Dorflinger for his 90th victory.

Nieto's passion and enthusiasm for racing meant that he was always destined to remain a key figure inside the paddock and an immensely popular one. He went into team management before becoming a hugely respected pundit and commentator for Spanish TV. He was honoured for his achievements in 2000 when he was made a MotoGP Legend. When Rossi equalled his 90 career victories, at Le Mans in 2008, Nieto famously celebrated by riding Rossi's Yamaha YZR-M1 machine with the Italian as pillion. In August 2017, the MotoGP paddock was plunged into mourning when Nieto died from injuries suffered in a road traffic accident in Ibiza.

Honda returned to the World Championship in 1982, after a limited introduction in 1979 of the revolutionary model NR500, a four-stroke that was probably ahead of its time but was a resounding failure. Honda ultimately embraced the two-stroke engine and won the 500cc title in 1983, with a young prodigy called Freddie Spencer. Americans and Australians

ruled the 500cc category for 20 years, with the sole exception of Marco Lucchinelli (1981) and Franco Uncini (1982).

The end of the eighties set the stage for another huge change. For 1990, the World Championship was reduced to only three categories: 125cc, 250cc and 500cc, plus sidecars, although this latter class slowly but surely lost importance. The premier class — the 500cc World Championship — suffered a crisis that reduced the number of its participants to an all-time low. Regulations were amended to raise the minimum weight for this category. Also, new formulas were devised to find new, affordable and competitive materials and to increase the number of riders.

Each manufacturer set its own course, but Honda made a key decision that became the basis for the 'democratization' of the premier class: the introduction of the 'big-bang' engine. The innovative NSR500, which Honda introduced in 1992, resulted from the company's creative engineering group searching for ways to use horsepower in a more manageable way, so that rear tyre grip was not compromised in the pursuit of power.

The more rider-friendly 'big-bang' motor revolutionised the 500cc era and the NSR500 dominated the latter stages of the premier-class two-stroke era, taking seven of the last 10 World Championship 500cc titles. Australian legend Mick Doohan was immediately enamoured with the NSR500 because its more forgiving nature allowed better corner exit acceleration and less wheelspin. The result was a reduction in the number of brutal 500cc high-sides that were such a common feature of that era.

By the eighties the evolution of motorsports had reached a level at which the FIM could no longer deny the growing evidence of the economic value of the World Championship, although the mere mention of this matter had long become taboo in many federation settings. Negotiations for television rights lasted several years until they were awarded in 1991 to the Spanish company Dorna, under the FIM presidency of Jos Vaessen. Dorna, which was virtually unknown in the motorcycle racing realm, took charge of television rights from 1992. Although not all the actors in the World Championship received this decision in the best spirit, Dorna's skilful actions averted a serious crisis.

ABOVE Ángel Nieto celebrates one of his 62 125cc Grand Prix wins en route to the 1979 World Championship title riding the Minarelli.

CHAPTER 5
1992–1996
INNOCENCE TO ACCOMPLISHMENT
BY MICHAEL SCOTT

The changes wrought to motorcycle grand prix racing between 1992 and 1996 were both pivotal and far-reaching, for at least two fundamental reasons.

One concerned the politics and the management. The revolution was over by the start of 1992; evolution of a new unified commercial and sporting entity began that same year. A tripartite union between the FIM, Bernie Ecclestone's Two Wheel Promotions (TWP) and Dorna was in control. There were some bumpy times, but long before 1996 TWP had gone, Ecclestone remained in the most distant of advisory roles, and Dorna had taken control. The structure of modern MotoGP was taking shape.

The other concerned the racing. The period began with the tail end of one golden age, a time when a group of superstars (mainly American, with some help from Australia) and a paddock full of fast-developing two-strokes meant a variety of winners. They generally came from that select group, but for years neither fans nor riders themselves could confidently predict the result of any race.

By the end of the period, it was vastly different. Most of that galaxy had departed — Lawson, Rainey, Schwantz, Gardner, Mamola.

Only one remained, and Mick Doohan rose head and shoulders above the competition. Now the difficulty was in predicting who might come second.

Technically, Honda had also seized the high ground.

RIGHT At Jerez in the 1992 Spanish Grand Prix Mick Doohan races from the line in front of Wayne Rainey and the Suzukis of Doug Chandler and Kevin Schwantz.

The company's insistence on independent thinking had seen some wrong turnings and pig-headed experiments in the past. The most important change came in 1992, with the arrival of the 'big-bang' engine with its close firing intervals. With a new, deeper exhaust drone, Honda rewrote the rules of tyre adhesion and took a clear stride ahead of the opposition. Throughout that year the rivals struggled to make their own 'big-bang' engines, Suzuki first, then Cagiva, then Yamaha. But reliability issues with the hastily contrived new engines kept Honda ahead.

A further process of logical refinement meant that at last, over the next five seasons, the once-unruly Honda NSR V4 was able to stay there. Or was it just the massive talent of Mighty Mick Doohan that made the NSR the definitive 500cc racing two-stroke? Doohan and Honda might have taken over earlier, but for a twist of circumstances in 1992.

The Australian had been second overall the year before, splitting the two great rivals, winner Wayne Rainey on the Marlboro Yamaha and the scintillating but too often erratic Kevin Schwantz on the Lucky Strike Suzuki. Come the 'big-bang' revolution of 1992, and

ABOVE Mick Doohan won the opening four Grands Prix of the 1992 season riding the 'big-bang' V4 Honda.

LEFT The 1992 Dutch TT turned that year's World Championship on its head and brought Álex Crivillé his first 500cc victory.

ABOVE Mick Doohan leads the 1992 Italian Grand Prix from Doug Chandler and Wayne Rainey.

RIGHT Mick Doohan's domination of the 1992 World Championship was shattered when he broke his leg in a practice crash at Assen.

Doohan won the first four races with apparent ease. His rivals took one win each thereafter, but Mick was second each time, and won again in Germany, to stretch his title lead over Schwantz to a massive 53 points. Rainey was adrift by another 12, and the Californian, furthermore, was absent through injury from the next race, Assen's showpiece Dutch TT. What could stop Doohan now?

Then it was his turn to crash in practice. He broke both bones in his left leg, and the injury was further complicated by controversially botched treatment in the local Dutch hospital. A problem turned into a disaster, with the real possibility that he might lose his leg.

There began two of the most classic fightbacks in racing history.

One was from Doohan, who missed the next three races while GP medic Dr Claudio Costa rescued him from hospital, halted the gangrene and saved his leg by sewing the two limbs together so they could share blood supply. Mick, looking like a ghost, returned to the penultimate round in Brazil, still leading on points, 22 ahead of Rainey, but far from competitive.

The other was from Rainey, who later said: "In racing, you should never give up, because anything can happen... and this year it did."

Shrugging his own injury aside, Wayne returned to win two of the remaining five races. The second was in Brazil, where Doohan struggled to 12th. At the last round, at Kyalami in South Africa, Rainey was third, Doohan sixth. Rainey was champion for a third year in a row, by just four points.

ABOVE Somehow Dr Claudio Costa not only saved Mick Doohan's leg but also got him fit to contest the last two Grands Prix of the 1992 season.

LEFT Wayne Rainey retained the 500cc world title in 1992 after finishing third at the final round in South Africa.

ABOVE Eddie Lawson brought Cagiva its historic first 500cc victory in the 1992 Hungarian Grand Prix.

BELOW Another Italian manufacturer emerged when Alessandro Gramigni brought Aprilia its first 125cc title in 1992.

Former 250 champion John Kocinski (Marlboro Yamaha) took that Kyalami win with Schwantz fifth, giving Kocinski third overall by three points ahead of the Suzuki superstar, with second Suzuki rider Doug Chandler a close fifth.

The 1992 season brought a long-awaited first win to Italian marque Cagiva, with four-times champion Eddie Lawson achieving that fulfilment in a canny race in mixed conditions in Hungary. More wins would follow in 1993, before the factory finally withdrew its red bikes at the end of 1994.

That year was also the swan-song of Wayne Gardner, pioneering Australian champion of 1987. His last season was interrupted by injuries (his place on the Rothmans Honda going to rising compatriot Daryl Beattie for several races), but marked by an emotional final fighting victory at Britain's Donington Park.

At the same time, a new initiative had boosted both numbers and hopes for midfield runners in the premier class, after dwindling numbers of competitive production racers had left those without factory contracts or lease deals short of available machinery. Yamaha provided V4 engines, while French firm

ROC and Britain's Harris Performance built chassis to Yamaha's design. Privateers now had close replicas of the previous year's factory Yamaha YZRs.

Honda prevailed in the 250 class as well, with a second title for Italy's Luca Cadalora, from Loris Reggiani and Pierfrancesco Chili, the best yet for the steadily improving new marque from Italy — Aprilia. A first-time winner also put himself on the map, 21-year-old Max Biaggi. He would prove increasingly important in the ensuing years. Another portent came in 125s, where Alessandro Gramigni won a first championship for Aprilia.

For 1993, with Dorna taking majority control after a share purchase of TWP, the Spanish company became able to address issues affecting the revised Grand Prix structure, and to find a way to cope with a variety of growing pains. One was falling crowd numbers, especially in Austria, Germany and Britain, with similar to follow after a return to the USA following a one-year hiatus. Those who stayed away missed a year of unusual variety. There were seven different premier-class race winners in 1993, matching the number in 250s and more than in the ever-lively 125 class.

Spain's growing influence was marked by a third GP on the Iberian peninsula, with Madrid's Jarama joining Jerez and Catalunya, a replacement for the cancelled South African round.

The year brought a long-awaited first title to Lucky Strike Suzuki and Kevin Schwantz, but in tragic circumstances. His career-long rival Wayne Rainey had

ABOVE Loris Capirossi celebrates his 250cc victory at the 1993 San Marino Grand Prix at Mugello.

LEFT In 1993 Kevin Schwantz delivered the 500cc world title for Suzuki in the most unfortunate of circumstances.

regained the points lead after Schwantz suffered mid-season injury, and Rainey seemed set for number four in a row when he crashed out of the lead at Misano, and suffered injuries that left him in a wheelchair.

"I'd much rather not be champion and for Wayne not to be injured," said Kevin. His own career would never recover: more injury spoiled his title defence in 1994; and he would quit abruptly early in 1995, bereft of further motivation, after nine brilliant years and 25 GP wins. Without Rainey to race against, it just wasn't the same for the swashbuckling Texan.

Until that cathartic moment, it had been a great year. Round three at Suzuka proved the point — the closest podium in history so far saw Rainey, Schwantz and Beattie (Yamaha, Suzuki and Honda) over the line inside 0.287 of a second.

Beattie was now full-time with Rothmans Honda alongside Doohan, who was still weak from his 1992 injury, with several surgical procedures still to follow. With Schwantz and Rainey taking four wins apiece, Luca Cadalora took two on the Marlboro Yamaha. There were one each for third-placed Beattie, Brazilian Alex Barros (Suzuki) and Kocinski, now on a Cagiva.

And just one win also for Doohan. This would change radically in the year to come. The 1993 season marked the end of an era: Schwantz was the last of a string of serial American World Champions; and a time of unpredictable results was over.

The 1993 250 series was close fought, with Japan's Tetsuya Harada (Yamaha) defeating Loris Capirossi's Honda by just four points to become the second of his nation to win a title in any class. The next best was again an Aprilia, with Loris Reggiani third; but Max Biaggi's switch to Honda had proved disappointing, finishing fourth. In the smallest class, diminutive German Dirk Raudies claimed a steadfast title win against a rising tide of Japanese talent.

There were many changes as 1994 began, and not all of them comfortable. One was the loss of major sponsor Rothmans to Formula One; the bigger surprise was that Honda was unable to replace them with a sponsor of sufficient stature. Instead the biggest Japanese brand embarked on a spell of almost complete domination by racing in its own factory colours.

Equally concerning was the increasing isolation of the premier racing class. Although ROC and Harris

BELOW Daryl Beattie arrived in the 500cc class in 1993 and won the German Grand Prix at Hockenheim.

Yamahas had addressed the shortage of machinery in the Grand Prix paddocks, there was no such relief for the lower echelons of racing, and one by one national championships had switched from traditional 500cc racing machines to the increasingly popular Superbikes, based on sporting four-stroke street bikes. The last to change was the most significant: the All-Japan national championship, supported directly by that country's major factories. In 1994 this switched to four-stroke Superbikes. The writing was on the wall for the magnificent but now ever-less-relevant 500cc two-stroke prototypes, although they would survive for another eight years.

The way the racing panned out over the coming seasons rather underlined the point. Mick Doohan's dominance was magnificent and the technical excellence of his Honda and its rivals also inspiring. But a lack of variety translated into a sort of sterility. A taint of stagnation would not go away.

Doohan's 1994 performance was very remarkable. Out of 14 rounds, the Australian won nine. Defender Schwantz won just two, his final victory, in Britain, achieved while wearing a plaster cast after yet another wrist injury, with the others going to Cadalora and Kocinski, who finished third overall in Cagiva's final and best-yet season. Doohan was in the top three at every race, and his winning margin over Cadalora was 143 points over the Italian's 174; he had almost doubled his closest rival's score.

Mick matched that record-winning margin again in 1997, when he beat team-mate Tady Okada; and the record would stand until Valentino Rossi defeated Max Biaggi by 140 points in 2002.

In between 1994 and 1998, Doohan won every title. He was truly a colossus, but accusations that racing had become a bit too predictable were hard to refute.

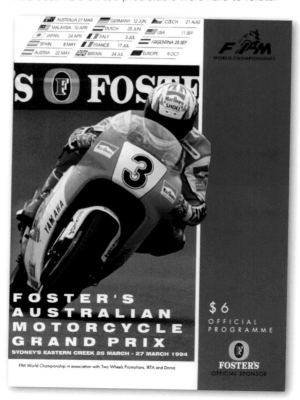

ABOVE Tetsuya Harada fought off Loris Capirossi to clinch the 1993 250cc World Championship.

LEFT At the opening round of the 1994 season at Eastern Creek in Australia John Kocinski brought Cagiva success.

ABOVE Cees Doorakkers in action on the 1994 Harris Yamaha that formed the very backbone of the 500cc World Championship.

BELOW From 1992 Yamaha provided factory 500cc race engines for installation in chassis designed and built by Harris.

"What do you want me to do?" asked Doohan defiantly. "Slow down?"

By the end of 1994 there was much uncertainty, with not only Dorna and the FIM each making contingency plans for its own all-new championship, but teams' association IRTA also threatening a breakaway. The arguments were resolved, but these were uneasy times.

There were, however, some fresh shoots. One was Aprilia's entry to the top class with a heretical lightweight 'super 250', taking advantage of a lower minimum weight for twin-cylinder bikes (100kg against 130kg for the fours). The bike, displacing just 400cc to retain the power characteristics of a 250, made a tentative start, but would inspire a significant imitator two years later from no less a presence than Honda.

By coincidence or fate, Doohan's big-class domination was matched in the 250 category. Max Biaggi had returned to Aprilia, and in 1994 took the first title for himself and the Italian bike. And again in 1995 and 1996, before switching to Honda in 1997 to do it again.

A different kind of three-year domination began in 125s, with three years of Japanese winners. Kazuto Sakata (Aprilia) took the 1994 crown, Haruchika Aoki

defeated Sakata in 1995 on a Honda; and in 1996 the top three were all Japanese – Honda's Aoki again, ahead of Masaki Tokudome and Tomomi Manako. By now, however, there was a new name and a first-time race winner — Valentino Rossi was ninth overall.

The 1995 season began with a significant change for the smaller classes — a new rule limiting riders to just one bike. Suggestions of adopting the same cost-cutting approach to the 500cc class had been rejected on the same grounds that the smaller classes had objected: safety (in case a crashed bike was too hastily patched up), fairness (should a rider lose his bike at the start of a crucial qualifying session) and finally, in the interests of the show, giving all riders a chance to run in every practice and qualifying session to ensure plenty for spectators to see.

Doohan was in control again, winning the first two of 13 races outright and adding another five victories. He finished off the podium just once — fourth in the final round in Barcelona — but, more remarkably, twice failed to score. In Jerez he crashed out of the lead at the same corner that in 1999 would ultimately end his career; and he fell again at the next race in Germany.

ABOVE At last the combination of Mick Doohan and the NSR Honda won the 500cc world title in 1994 and embarked on their period of total domination in the premier class.

BELOW Kazuto Sakata won the 1994 125cc world title with Aprilia after finishing second the previous year.

ABOVE In 1994 Max
Biaggi won the first of
his four consecutive
250cc world titles, the first
three coming on Aprilias.

GRAND PRIX
DEUTSCHLAND

NÜRBURGRING 19·21·5·95

FIM
WORLD CHAMPIONSHIPS

AUSTRALIA	26 · 3	ITALY	11 · 6	RIO	17 · 9
MALAYSIA	2 · 4	HOLLAND	24 · 6	ARGENTINA	24 · 9
JAPAN	23 · 4	FRANCE	9 · 7	CATALUNYA	8 · 10
SPAIN	7 · 5	BRITAIN	23 · 7		
GERMANY	21 · 5	CZECH REPUBLIC	20 · 8		

OFIZIELLES
PROGRAMM

10 DM

FIM WORLD CHAMPIONSHIPS IN ASSOCIATION WITH TWO WHEEL PROMOTIONS, RPA AND DORNA.

RIGHT The German
Grand Prix programme
of 1995 — in this period
the venue kept switching
between Hockenheim and
the new Nürburgring.

This meant his margin over second-placed compatriot
Beattie, now on a Lucky Strike Suzuki, was a relatively
tame 33 points. Beattie won two races and third-placed
Cadalora (Marlboro Yamaha) also took two.

Spaniard Alberto Puig (Honda) was a first-time winner,
but his subsequent career would be spoiled by injury;
after retirement he became a leading light in recruiting
and training young riders. Doohan's factory Honda team-
mate Álex Crivillé, the former 125cc champion who in
1999 would become Spain's first premier-class World
Champion, won his second 500cc Grand Prix.

Kevin Schwantz started the year slowly, then an
uncharacteristically lacklustre performance in the rain
at Suzuka — at a track and in conditions where he
had previously often been unbeatable — revealed an
incurable malaise. "I wasn't having any fun doing it. I
was racing because everybody else thought I should be
racing. I wasn't doing it for myself any more." He missed
the next two races, then announced his premature
retirement in Italy. Dorna later retired his number '34'
from the premier class as a mark of respect shared by
fans and rivals alike.

For 1996, again, Doohan was unstoppable. Eight race

ABOVE Alberto Puig won the 1995 Spanish Grand Prix at Jerez to become the first Spanish winner of a 500cc race on home soil.

LEFT Luca Cadalora beat Mick Doohan in the 1995 Brazilian Grand Prix in Rio, but the Australian gained revenge a week later in Argentina.

wins out of 15, but while his margin over team-mate Crivillé was a comfortable 64 points, there was plenty of proof that the Honda — which took the top four title positions and eight times locked out the podium — was a super-strong contender not only for the Australian. His stranglehold on the top-three podium was less assured than previously, with fifth and sixth placings now and then; while the honour of taking Honda's 100th premier-class race victory went to first-time winner Carlos Checa. Crivillé, who had won his first 500cc Grand Prix in Assen four years earlier, was developing all the time and a classic 0.002 second victory in Brno over Doohan after he had stalked him all race fuelled the fire between the two team-mates.

Cadalora, now on an independent Honda in a white fairing, took two race wins, and was third overall; Crivillé also won twice; Checa just the once.

The other two wins went to first-timers on Yamahas. Norick Abe won a popular classic at home in Japan and ex-125 and 250 champion Loris Capirossi took the last round in Australia, riding for Wayne Rainey in his role as team manager.

The Aprilia 400cc twin was far behind, with Doriano

Romboni 19th overall. But the idea had born fruit for Honda, with Tadayuki Okada campaigning their own prototype V-twin, a full 500, and destined for a production-racer future. Okada was on pole at the first round in Malaysia, finished second in Australia and was twice third. In the end, though, the twin flattered to deceive.

There were other threats to Japan's V4 hegemony. One was a technically interesting European engine, branded Elf. It was also a V4, but very different, with spaced-out crankpins (big ends) making it effectively a flat-four 'Boxer', with pairs of cylinders sharing the same crankcase volume and firing simultaneously. Another was being readied for 1997: a three-cylinder two-stroke vee built to the orders of former hero and successful Yamaha team owner Kenny Roberts, which would race under the name Modenas, and later Proton.

Stagnation was being swept aside.

It had been half a decade when the only stability had been the leading engine designs — and latterly the domination of Doohan. Other changes, especially political and in racing management, had been profound.

And that was just the start of it.

ABOVE Valentino Rossi won his first Grand Prix in the 1996 Czech Republic 125cc race at Brno.

LEFT Boy wonder. Baby-faced Valentino Rossi arrived to put Grand Prix motorcycle racing in a place it had never been to previously.

CHAPTER 6
1997–2001
ROSSI ARRIVES
BY MATTHEW MILES

During the five-year stretch from 1997 to 2001, Grand Prix racing's premier class was in transition, although few, even those intimate with the sport, likely realized what they were witnessing. Mick Doohan, Álex Crivillé, Kenny Roberts Jr and Valentino Rossi took top honours, with Doohan and Rossi bookending the era with five successive championships apiece, a feat not since replicated.

Doohan arrived at Shah Alam in Malaysia for round one of the 1997 season with three titles already under his belt. During those three years, the Australian finished first in more than half of the races he started — 24 in total. In 1997 he won another 12, including 10 in a row, and completed the 15 rounds with 143

more points than runner-up Tadayuki Okada. Honda won every race and dominated the final standings, taking the top five spots.

Pundits credited Doohan's supremacy to four qualities: he was the fittest, hardest working, most determined and fastest.

The motorcycles — a mix of twins, triples and fours — were part of this transition. At Shah Alam, Doohan rode an NSR500 outwardly identical to his 1996 winner but internally different. Honda had ditched the 'big-bang' V4 for the prior 'Screamer' that fired its pairs of cylinders in 180-degree intervals. Port timing, however, was similar to that of the 'big-bang' and gave the good torque while re-establishing lost feel for the rear tyre.

"It's a big mistake to compare this engine with the one from 1991," Doohan cautioned. "I wanted to try the old firing order because that always seemed to have a more direct connection between the throttle and the back tyre. You could control the slide more and it would over-rev to sustain the wheelspin, whereas the 'big-bang' would run into a brick wall, and the tyre would hook up when you didn't want it to."

In Malaysia Doohan broke the lap record set seven years earlier by John Kocinski on a Yamaha. "I didn't have to spin the tyre to get away from the other guys," he said. Motivation also factored into Doohan's decision to switch power plants. "It really is more fun to ride, and that is important for me," he admitted. "But make no mistake, if it turns out later that there's some disadvantage to it, I'll be straight back on the 'big-bang'."

At this stage of his career, Crivillé already had five years of 500cc GP experience, with four victories to his credit. Roberts Jr was beginning his second season in the top category, albeit aboard the rushed-to-grid Modenas KR3, not the Yamaha YZR500 on which

RIGHT Indonesia staged its second, and last, Grand Prix in 1997 at Sentul.

ABOVE Tadayuki Okada leads team-mates Mick Doohan, Álex Crivillé and Takuma Aoki in 1997 at Mugello.

LEFT Honda rule: the impressive line-up of (from left) Takuma Aoki, Álex Crivillé, Mick Doohan and Tadayuki Okada won all 15 Grands Prix in 1997.

RIGHT Nobuatsu Aoki on his way to third place at Mugello in 1997.

BELOW Mick Doohan was unbeatable in 1997 and won 12 Grands Prix to secure his fourth world title with ease.

he made his premier-class début. While Crivillé and Roberts Jr witnessed Doohan's domination first-hand, Rossi was busy destroying the 125cc ranks.

The young Italian was not the only talent making waves in the smaller-displacement classes. Max Biaggi won the 1997 250cc title, his fourth successively in the class. Kazuto Sakata took top 125cc honours the following year, and Loris Capirossi beat Rossi in the middleweight class. In 1999, a winless but consistent Emilio Alzamora and a dominant Rossi collected the 125 and 250 crowns.

Roberts Jr grew up in the GP paddock. Ex-racer and distinguished engineer Warren Willing had known Roberts Jr since he was four and worked for his father, three-time 500cc World Champion Kenny Roberts. "Because of his situation, Junior was learning the right way of doing things," Willing said. "He wasn't left to his own devices to just wander through and figure out how to ride. It was there in front of him to watch and listen.

"Kenny Senior got a lot of flak because he made things available. In 1991, we were testing at Laguna Seca with Wayne Rainey. That was the first time Junior rode a 250 on a race track — he was running around while we were testing the 500. When we were at Phillip Island with Rainey and Luca Cadalora, Kenny had an extra bike and Junior rode it at his pace. Those opportunities weren't available to most people."

Roberts Jr spent 1997 and 1998 on the Modenas KR3 triple designed by Bud Aksland, Mike Sinclair and Willing, and made reality with Malaysian funding by Tom Walkinshaw Racing. In two seasons — the first on Michelins, the second on Dunlops — Roberts Jr had nine top-10 finishes, including a best of sixth in Germany after starting from the front row, but failed to crack the top 12 overall in either campaign.

That experience was not lost on Roberts Jr. "I gained as much knowledge that would have taken four years anywhere else," he said. "We developed a lot of stuff. We used two makes of tyres in two years, which gave me a lot of feel. I learned a lot of what makes a motorcycle do what it does and how to describe it. I also established a close relationship with Warren."

Roberts Jr was one of many riders who benefited from his father's exhaustive know-how and international reach. In addition to hosting young talent at his rural California digs, Roberts Sr introduced dirt track to Spain through the Kenny Roberts Training Ranch outside of the Circuit of Catalunya. Crivillé was one of the high-profile stars who turned to Roberts to improve his throttle-control skills.

"Riding the Rotax 600 at the Roberts school helped me stay calm and comfortable when the NSR500 was

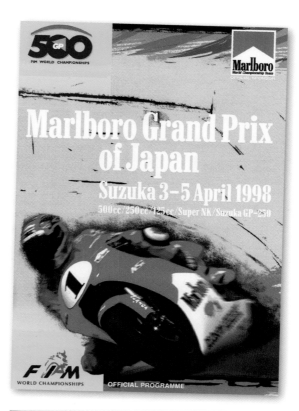

LEFT & BELOW Max Biaggi made a sensational 500cc début in 1998 when he won the Japanese Grand Prix at Suzuka.

ABOVE Carlos Checa scored his second 500cc victory and on home soil at the 1998 Community of Madrid Grand Prix in Jarama.

RIGHT Kenny Roberts Jr continued his Grand Prix education in 1998 on his father's Modenas 500cc machine with sponsorship from Malaysia.

spinning and sliding under acceleration to get the bike turned and the power down earlier," Crivillé said. "I was racing Mick Doohan on the same bikes, and riding dirt track helped me get on his level in spite of coming from a 125cc and 250 background."

Eight wins in 14 starts notwithstanding, Doohan viewed 1998 — the first year for torque-robbing no-lead fuel — as an "up-and-down season". After five rounds, Crivillé had a two-point edge, with Japanese GP winner Biaggi third. At Jarama, Doohan was on pole for the fourth time but crashed in turn one after contact with Simon Crafar. At Brno, he slid off chasing Biaggi. The defending champion left the Czech Republic third in the points.

Doohan won at Imola, leading Crivillé and Biaggi home, but Catalunya was the turning point. Biaggi had the championship lead, with Doohan second, four points down. Crivillé — third in points, seven behind Biaggi — started from pole, with Biaggi, Alex Barros and Doohan completing the front row. Crivillé never got past turn one, torpedoed in a chain collision begun by Katsuaki Fujiwara that also claimed Jean-Michel Bayle.

Crivillé picked up his smashed NSR and rejoined the

ABOVE Álex Crivillé started the European part of the 1998 season in brilliant style by winning his home Spanish Grand Prix at Jerez.

LEFT Álex Crivillé became the first Spanish 500cc World Champion in 1999.

ABOVE Kenny Roberts Jr became a real championship threat in 1999 with four Grand Prix wins on the Suzuki.

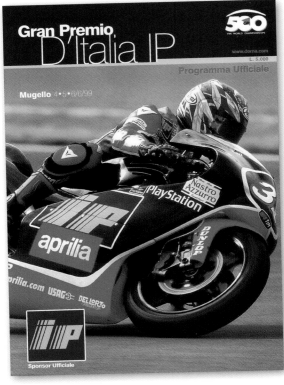

RIGHT In the nineties Mugello became the regular home of the Italian Grand Prix and it has remained there ever since.

race only to complete one lap. Bayle stood briefly then collapsed. Fifteen laps later, leaders Biaggi and Barros were penalized for passing under a waved yellow at the beginning of lap two. Barros pitted to serve his 10-second stop-and-go, but Biaggi stubbornly continued racing and was disqualified. Doohan took 25 points, with his next-closest title rival, Carlos Checa, sixth.

With that, Doohan was back in control of the championship. At Phillip Island, the Australian "broke the tow" on cold tyres and won again. In Argentina, he repeated at the top — the first time he had won the final race of the season. Crivillé, second on points, opted for a Screamer engine. He crashed, handing fifth and the runner-up slot in the standings to Biaggi. "I am very angry with myself," Crivillé said.

Doohan and Crivillé worked out of the same garage for three full seasons. "There was always a very competitive atmosphere, but it was professional," Crivillé said, noting there were some tense moments, too. Like the time in 1996 when Crivillé rear-ended Doohan at Eastern Creek in Australia, taking both riders out of victory contention. "After that," he said, "we were much more rivals than team-mates."

Honda lost its star rider at the third race of the 1999 season. Doohan began his fifth successive title defence by finishing fourth in the opening round in Malaysia and second in Japan. During qualifying at Jerez, he crashed at 120-plus mph, breaking his right shoulder and leg, and left wrist. Surgeons inserted two plates and 12 screws in his leg, and a plate in his left forearm.

Asked what he would do without racing, Doohan said, "I'll miss it, but I won't be depressed. I accomplished what I set out to do. I've always had that in front of me, and now it will be behind me. I'm 35 years old. I'm not an old man, but I'm old for my sport. I know the next 15 years will go quickly, and then I'll be 50. Another 30 and I'll be 80, and that about sums it up."

With sixth victories, four consecutively, Crivillé took top honours that season — "the year the doors were opened for Spaniards," Dani Pedrosa would later say — 11 years after he won the 125cc title. The quiet Catalan was Spain's first 500cc race winner and first (and only) 500cc World Champion. Countering the Honda stranglehold, Roberts Jr, now on a Suzuki, won four races, including the first two, and was second in the points.

"Kenny was 100 per cent confident that he could ride as fast as anyone — even, at that time, Mick Doohan — provided he had a competitive bike," Willing said. Roberts Jr added, "If you look at the last 10 years of GP racing, nobody had been able to jump on a 500

ABOVE **Father and son World Champions — Kenny Roberts Jr and Sr.**

LEFT **Valentino Rossi and crew chief Jerry Burgess get ready for Rossi's 500cc début in 2000 at Welkom in South Africa.**

RIGHT The King and his successor — Mick Doohan retired in 1999 and Rossi arrived in the premier class one year later.

BELOW Valentino Rossi crashed out of his first 500cc Grand Prix in South Africa but that first win was not far away.

and walk the walk. Our goal was to beat Mick, and we did that right away. He absolutely dominated for five years, winning five titles. Then he fell down in Spain and was done."

Roberts Jr had been on Suzuki's wish list since 1997. "We never realized how good Kevin Schwantz was until he wasn't around any more," Suzuki team manager Garry Taylor said about the 1993 500cc World Champion. Tadeo Shigenoya green-lighted the programme. "Mr. Shigenoya was retiring," Taylor said. "He was given one last project: put the GP team back on course."

Willing joined Roberts Jr at Suzuki. "When we tested the bike at the end of 1998," he said, "I had a fair idea of its performance level and problems that I saw other riders having with it. The basic layout was similar to what we had with the Yamaha, and the experience building the Modenas gave us insight into other areas. Suzuki wanted to win the championship in 2000, but there was a lot of work to do.

"We worked on areas that we could influence quickly. The engine was the weakest point. Compared to the Yamahas that we ran in 1996, the Suzuki was

ABOVE Australian Garry McCoy was a crowd favourite with his flamboyant riding and he took three Grand Prix wins in 2000.

LEFT Valentino Rossi's first 500cc victory came in the 2000 British Grand Prix at Donington Park.

ABOVE Norick Abe
was a popular winner
of his home Japanese
Grand Prix at Suzuka
in 2000.

BELOW Post-race press
conference at Suzuka 2000
with winner Norick Abe
flanked by Kenny Roberts Jr
(left) and Tadayuki Okada.

Suzuka 2000

down about 20bhp at 10,000rpm. The bike was good under brakes, but not particularly good on corners that turned back on themselves — it tended to understeer and run wide in the middle of those turns — and didn't offer a great deal of feedback."

A week before the first Grand Prix of 2000 in South Africa, Willing's wife, Wendy, was diagnosed with cancer. Roberts Jr and Willing were on the grid at Phakisa. "There wasn't anything physically I could do," said Willing, who lost his own battle with the disease in 2015. "Wendy was aware how much work we put into everything and had watched Kenny grow up and mature as a rider and a person. It was his shot."

Roberts Jr won four times and scored points everywhere but Assen, where a failed piston threw him skyward. That weekend, Crivillé — battling a more powerful but less rideable engine — finally got a front-row start and was second behind Barros. Rossi, guided by ex-Doohan crew chief Jeremy Burgess, understood the NSR500 in the second half of the calendar and tallied two wins and 10 podiums for second overall. Crivillé was ninth.

When Rossi first arrived in the premier class, he

ABOVE Brazilian Alex Barros won his first Grand Prix for seven years with victory at Assen in 2000.

LEFT Kenny Roberts Jr clinched his historic 500cc world title in Brazil after a calculated sixth place at Rio.

ABOVE Max Biaggi, Valentino Rossi, Loris Capirossi and Jürgen van der Goorbergh race from the start line at Brno in 2001.

BELOW Former 125cc and 250cc World Champion Loris Capirossi in action on the Honda. His MotoGP career really kicked off when he joined Ducati.

OPPOSITE Valentino Rossi celebrates victory at the 2001 British Grand Prix at Donington Park on the way to his first 500cc world title.

tested Doohan's old NSR. "It was difficult but quite good to ride," he said. "When I rode the new engine that Honda prepared for Crivillé, we had a lot of problems. The bike was fast but impossible to ride." Burgess added, "At the end of 1999, they'd asked Crivillé as a World Champion what he wanted, and he said, 'I want more power.' So they gave him more power."

That is true, Crivillé now admits. "Yamaha and Suzuki had caught up and had about the same power as Honda." Roberts Jr, meanwhile, made the most from his unique situation. "Kenny knew precisely what the bike would do, precisely what the tyres could do, and precisely what he could do," Willing said. "Kenny took every point that we were capable of producing."

After "doing what was necessary" in Brazil to wrap up the title — a first for a father and son — Roberts decimated the field in Japan, beating Rossi by more than six seconds. "Kenny says he didn't realize until after the finish of the Rio race the pressure that he was carrying," Willing said. "He was thinking, 'Should I go for it or not?' At that level, you can't hesitate. Once it was over, he said, 'Wait until the next race.'"

ABOVE Max Biaggi finally had to settle for second place in the 2001 World Championship after some bitter battles with Rossi on and off the track.

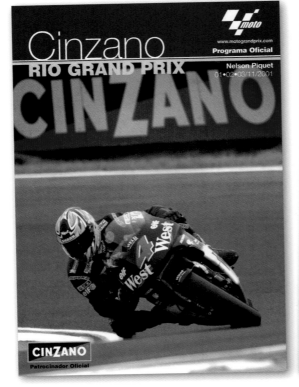

RIGHT Alex Barros was on the programme cover for his home Grand Prix at Rio in 2001, the last race of the 500cc World Championship era.

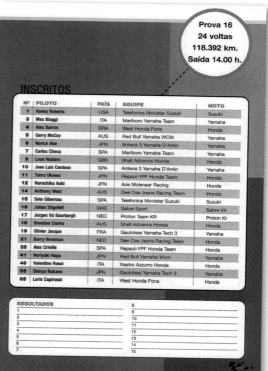

Cinzano
RIO GRAND PRIX

moto
www.motograndprix.com
Programa Oficial
Nelson Piquet
01•02•03/11/2001

CINZANO

CINZANO
Patrocinador Oficial

Prova 16
24 voltas
118.392 km.
Saída 14.00 h.

INSCRITOS

Nº	PILOTO	PAÍS	EQUIPE	MOTO
1	Kenny Roberts	USA	Telefonica Movistar Suzuki	Suzuki
3	Max Biaggi	ITA	Marlboro Yamaha Team	Yamaha
4	Alex Barros	BRA	West Honda Pons	Honda
5	Garry McCoy	AUS	Red Bull Yamaha WCM	Yamaha
6	Norick Abe	JPN	Antena 3 Yamaha D'Antin	Yamaha
7	Carlos Checa	SPA	Marlboro Yamaha Team	Yamaha
9	Leon Haslam	GBR	Shell Advance Honda	Honda
10	Jose Luis Cardoso	SPA	Antena 3 Yamaha D'Antin	Yamaha
11	Tohru Ukawa	JPN	Repsol-YPF Honda Team	Honda
12	Haruchika Aoki	JPN	Arie Molenaar Racing	Honda
14	Anthony West	AUS	Dee Cee Jeans Racing Team	Honda
15	Sete Gibernau	SPA	Telefonica Movistar Suzuki	Suzuki
16	Johan Stigefelt	SWE	Sabre Sport	Sabre V4
17	Jurgen Vd Goorbergh	NED	Proton Team KR	Proton Kr
18	Brendan Clarke	AUS	Shell Advance Honda	Honda
19	Olivier Jacque	FRA	Gauloises Yamaha Tech 3	Yamaha
21	Barry Veneman	NED	Dee Cee Jeans Racing Team	Yamaha
28	Alex Criville	SPA	Repsol-YPF Honda Team	Honda
41	Noriyuki Haga	JPN	Red Bull Yamaha Wcm	Yamaha
46	Valentino Rossi	ITA	Nastro Azzurro Honda	Honda
56	Shinya Nakano	JPN	Gauloises Yamaha Tech 3	Yamaha
65	Loris Capirossi	ITA	West Honda Pons	Honda

RESULTADOS

1	8
2	9
3	10
4	11
5	12
6	13
7	14
	15

Rossi was looking toward the future, as well. "At Phillip Island, Valentino raced a completely new motorcycle, the 2001 NSR500," Roberts Jr said. "He told me that it was down on middle power but everything else was better. I said, 'Suzuki is going to have a new bike, too.' But when we got to the first test in Spain, the bike was the same — the same bike we knew wasn't competitive."

As the 20th century came to a close, Frenchman Olivier Jacque and Italian Roberto Locatelli were the top 125cc and 250 points earners. Daijiro Kato and Manuel Poggiali won the first 125 and 250 championships of the third Millennium. While Biaggi and Capirossi would reach the top step of the podium in Grand Prix racing's premier class, only Rossi would capture the title.

Rossi won 11 of 16 GPs in 2001, his climb to the top following a pattern: a year to learn, champion the following season. Crivillé retired at the end of 2001 with 20 victories and two world titles. Roberts Jr raced six and a half more years, five with Suzuki, but never won again. Rossi was only getting started. For the rider many now consider the greatest of all time, the four-stroke revolution would provide new challenges.

ABOVE Daijiro Kato celebrates with the Gresini team after sealing the 2001 250cc World Championship in Malaysia.

BELOW Manuel Poggiali finally overcame the spirited Youichi Ui to win the 125cc World Championship for Gilera.

CHAPTER 7
2002–2006
THE SOUND OF CHANGE
BY STEFANO SARAGONI

The reigning World Champion, Valentino Rossi, was the best-equipped rider on the 2002 grid, a year in which the old 500cc two-strokes raced alongside the new 1,000cc four-strokes to ensure adequate grids. The two-strokes, however, had no chance against the new machines with double the cylinder capacity.

Apart from Honda, there were no constructors really able to immediately afford the new rules of the MotoGP class, and the biggest motorcycle company in the world showed all of its technical muscle with the introduction of the RC211V and its five-cylinder engine. On his first ride in 2001, Rossi disliked the RC211V, but at the first winter test his attitude changed and thereafter he never repeated his previous opinion that

he would have preferred riding his beloved NSR500 two-stroke.

Valentino won the first race in Japan, but in South Africa, enjoying huge slides in every corner, he finally made the mistake that allowed Tohru Ukawa to win. That was a welcome gift for his team-mate, the only other rider — for the moment — on an RC211V. Then Valentino won seven races in a row and soon there was no doubt about the identity of the first four-stroke champion. Not until the Czech Republic Grand Prix, in August, was there a Yamaha win, courtesy of Max Biaggi, Honda's rival having started the season with a four-stroke engine of reduced capacity (942cc rather than the full 990cc) and still using carburettors.

RIGHT There were nine four-stroke machines in the entry list for the historic 2002 Japanese Grand Prix.

No.	ライダー Rider		年齢 Age	国籍/所属県 Nationality		マシン Machine	チーム Team
3	マックス・ビアッジ	Max BIAGGI	30	イタリア	ITA	YAMAHA	Marlboro Yamaha Team
4	アレックス・バロス	Alex BARROS	31	ブラジル	BRA	HONDA	West Honda Pons
6	阿部 典史	Norick ABE	26	東京	JPN	YAMAHA	Antena 3 Yamaha D'Antin
7	カルロス・チェカ	Carlos CHECA	29	スペイン	SPA	YAMAHA	Marlboro Yamaha Team
8	ギャリー・マッコイ	Garry McCOY	29	オーストラリア	AUS	YAMAHA	Red Bull Yamaha WCM
9	青木 宣篤	Nobuatsu AOKI	30	群馬	JPN	PROTON KR3	Proton Team KR
10	ケニー・ロバーツ	Kenny ROBERTS	28	アメリカ	USA	SUZUKI	Telefonica Movistar Suzuki
11	宇川 徹	Tohru UKAWA	28	千葉	JPN	HONDA	Repsol Honda Team
15	セテ・ジベルノー	Sete GIBERNAU	29	スペイン	SPA	SUZUKI	Telefonica Movistar Suzuki
17	ユルゲン・ファンデン・グールベルグ	Jurgen VD GOORBERGH	32	オランダ	NED	HONDA	Kanemoto Racing
19	オリビエ・ジャック	Olivier JACQUE	28	フランス	FRA	YAMAHA	Gauloises Yamaha Tech 3
20	ペレ・リバ	Pere RIBA	32	スペイン	SPA	YAMAHA	Antena 3 Yamaha D'Antin
21	ジョン・ホプキンス	John HOPKINS	18	アメリカ	USA	YAMAHA	Red Bull Yamaha WCM
31	原田 哲也	Tetsuya HARADA	31	千葉	JPN	HONDA	Pramac Honda Racing Team
33	梁 明	Akira RYO	34	東京	JPN	SUZUKI	Telefonica Movistar Suzuki
46	バレンティーノ・ロッシ	Valentino ROSSI	23	イタリア	ITA	HONDA	Repsol Honda Team
55	レジス・ラコーニ	Regis LACONI	26	フランス	FRA	APRILIA	MS Aprilia Racing
56	中野 真矢	Shinya NAKANO	24	千葉	JPN	YAMAHA	Gauloises Yamaha Tech 3
65	ロリス・カピロッシ	Loris CAPIROSSI	29	イタリア	ITA	HONDA	West Honda Pons
72	伊藤 真一	Shinichi ITOH	35	宮城	JPN	HONDA	Team HRC
74	加藤 大治郎	Daijiro KATOH	25	埼玉	JPN	HONDA	Fortuna Honda Gresini
99	ジェレミー・マックウィリアムス	Jeremy McWILLIAMS	38	イギリス	GBR	PROTON KR3	Proton Team KR

Entry List MotoGP Class
Start 4/7 Sun 14:00～
21 Laps(122.241km)
No. of Entries (エントリー台数) 22

昨年まで、500ccクラスと呼ばれてきたロードレース最高峰クラスだが、今年から、4ストロークエンジンに限り、最大排気量990ccまでが認められることになった。これにより、この最高峰クラスはMotoGPクラスへと呼称変更された。なお、エントリーリストにあるゼッケンが赤数字のライダーは、4ストロークMotoGPマシンによるエントリーとなる。

ABOVE History in the making — the four-stroke era begins with the start of the 2002 Japanese Grand Prix at Suzuka.

LEFT Riding the four-stroke RC211V Honda, Valentino Rossi carried on in 2002 where he had left off in 2001, winning at Suzuka.

RIGHT Tohru Ukawa inflicted a rare defeat on Honda team-mate Valentino Rossi in the 2002 South African Grand Prix.

BELOW The four-stroke Yamahas of Max Biaggi and Carlos Checa struggled against the Hondas in 2002 and the company had to wait until Brno for Biaggi to secure its first win of the year.

Rossi confirmed his title in Brazil, with four rounds
still to go. At that point Honda decided to support
the Pons team with an RC211V for Brazilian rider Alex
Barros. Those last four Grands Prix became known
as the *Mundialito*, with head-to-head confrontations
between Rossi and Barros providing interesting stories
for the media. At Motegi Barros was first and Rossi
second; Biaggi beat both of them at Sepang; Rossi won
from Barros at Phillip Island; and Barros beat Rossi again
in Valencia. Barros was the victor of the *Mundialito*.
These four races convinced Yamaha to make the
Brazilian an offer for 2003 that he accepted.

By 2003 there were no more 500s on the grid.
Ducati joined the fray, and the Italian bike immediately
showed its potential when, in the opening race at
Suzuka, Loris Capirossi got on the podium with Rossi
and Biaggi, who after four years with Yamaha was back
on a private Honda. Nobody knew it then, but this
would be the last Japanese Grand Prix at Suzuka, due
to the terrible accident in which Daijiro Kato hit the wall,
sadly dying in hospital some days later. The loss of Kato
weighed heavily on the hearts and minds of everybody
in the close-knit MotoGP community.

The South African Grand Prix at Welkom, the
first race after Kato's death, was incredible. Sete
Gibernau, his team-mate, seemed guided from heaven
and Rossi had no chance of beating him that day.
Gibernau's emotional win was a fitting tribute to his
late team-mate. In due course the Spaniard would
play a pivotal role in ensuring that MotoGP would do

**ABOVE The end of the
2002 season saw some
stirring battles between
Alex Barros and Valentino
Rossi, the Brazilian winning
two of the last four races.**

**LEFT Valentino Rossi
secured the first MotoGP
title with victory in Rio
with four rounds to go.**

everything in its power to make the sport safer after Kato's tragic passing.

It was at Welkom, under a rather ramshackle white awning, that Dorna CEO Carmelo Ezpeleta called a special summit attended by the entire MotoGP grid to discuss ways in which the sport could be made as safe as feasibly possible. Although there had always been open dialogue and clear communication between Dorna and the riders on a wide range of matters, including the paramount issue of safety, Ezpeleta was determined to introduce a more permanent and recognised platform where problems could be debated and solutions found.

The meeting may have taken place in modest surroundings, but the outcome was the formation of a powerful body that still plays an essential role in today's MotoGP World Championship. Little did anyone realise at the time, but that meeting in South Africa was the first of the Safety Commission that still convenes at every single Grand Prix on the Friday after practice. Four riders — Gibernau, Rossi, Kenny Roberts Jr and Nobuatsu Aoki — were elected to meet Ezpeleta at every round, while any rider from any class could attend the meetings to observe discussions.

OPPOSITE An inspired Sete Gibernau paid the ultimate tribute to Daijiro Kato, his lost team-mate, with victory at Welkom in 2003.

ABOVE Loris Capirossi brought Ducati its first premier-class victory in the 2003 Grand Prix of Catalunya.

BELOW Sete Gibernau honoured his late team-mate Daijiro Kato at the 2003 South African Grand Prix.

RIGHT The Catalunya
organisers chose the right
bike, Ducati, for their 2003
programme cover but they
did not predict the winning
rider — this is Troy Bayliss.

Gran Premi Marlboro de Catalunya

Catalunya 13-15/06 2003

BELOW Max Biaggi's first
victory of 2003 came in
the British Grand Prix at
Donington Park.

Starting at Welkom, Gibernau's performances
changed completely. He became more consistent,
and ended the championship in second place after
taking three more wins. Considering that Rossi seemed
unbeatable, that was a great achievement. Ducati very
quickly took its first Grand Prix win, in only the sixth
round at Catalunya, and Capirossi ended the year fourth
in the standings, behind Biaggi.

Yamaha had a disastrous year, with both its riders,
Checa and Barros, winless and only seventh and ninth
respectively in the points. Barros, who had been such
a star the previous year, became almost invisible and
could do no better than third place at Le Mans.

Drastic change was in the air. At the end of 2003,
in Valencia, Honda and Valentino Rossi announced the
end of their four-year partnership after three World
Championship crowns and 33 race wins. Rossi made
the difficult — but exciting — choice to join Yamaha,
choosing the bike that no other top riders wanted.
It seemed a huge gamble, but for Rossi it was an
opportunity to display his star quality by proving that he
did not need a Honda in order to win.

Yamaha was desperate for Rossi to spearhead its

challenge to win back the crown that had eluded the Japanese factory since 1992 and the last of Wayne Rainey's glorious three titles. Aware of Rossi's unease at Honda's arrogance that they could win without his special talent, the Italian was never more open to a shock move.

Honda negotiated tirelessly with Rossi and his management to keep their prized asset, but ultimately it was a doomed mission. Numerous covert meetings took place throughout the year between Rossi and Yamaha management, including Lin Jarvis and Davide Brivio.

The biggest shake-up witnessed in the sport for many years was confirmed just hours after Rossi won the season's final race in Valencia. In a packed press conference, and flanked by senior HRC management including Sporting Director Carlo Fiorani, Rossi announced he was leaving. Licking their wounds and being acutely aware of the threat Rossi would pose at Yamaha, Honda immediately barred him from testing his new machine until the following January, at the first official test in Malaysia.

As well as Rossi, Yamaha had another secret weapon. In the end it was the persuasive and

ABOVE Valentino Rossi and Honda went their separate ways at the end of 2003.

BELOW Valentino Rossi's first race for Yamaha, at Welkom in South Africa, saw an intense battle with Max Biaggi.

RIGHT Valentino Rossi made a sensational Yamaha début, beating Max Biaggi to win at Welkom in 2004.

BELOW LEFT Valentino Rossi savours that maiden Yamaha victory with second-placed Max Biaggi (left) and third-placed Sete Gibernau.

BELOW RIGHT Makoto Tamada celebrated being on the front of the 2004 Motegi programme by winning his home race.

charismatic Masao Furusawa who had convinced Rossi to join Yamaha. Furusawa quickly earned Rossi's trust and became almost like a father figure to him. He delivered clear thinking, a passionate work ethic and a strong will to succeed, all of which, when paired with Rossi's phenomenal riding skills, would form an incredibly potent combination.

Furusawa implemented a radical overhaul of Yamaha's race department to make sure everything behind the scenes was in place for an immediate attack on the title. He was also an engineering genius who dared to break with Yamaha's five-valve technology and instead prepare a crossplane-crankshaft bike with four valves per cylinder that Rossi immediately felt was capable of being a contender.

At the end of winter testing, Rossi was the undoubted favourite for the coming season and the world awaited the South African Grand Prix at Welkom. The race was one of the most sensational of all time, with an unbelievable duel for victory between Biaggi on the Honda and Rossi on his new Yamaha. The Honda was faster and more stable, but Rossi was ready to lose all to win. Inspired, Valentino rode

ABOVE & LEFT Valentino Rossi won the first Grand Prix in China at a wet Shanghai circuit in 2005.

through all problems and came out the winner.

This race virtually decided the championship because Rossi and the Yamaha team gained so much strength from it that the rest of the season became easier for them. In Rossi's wake, Gibernau was second in the standings, Biaggi third and Barros — back on a Honda — fourth.

As in the two previous years, the first race of the 2005 season had terrific meaning. This time the venue was in Spain, at Jerez, and after really impressive winter tests Sete Gibernau, riding Team Gresini's Honda, wanted to confirm to himself, Honda and the entire world that he was the man who could beat Valentino Rossi. The race was a great joust between them and the Spaniard put everything into it, and a bit more. On the last lap he led, but with Rossi on his shoulder. At the last corner, a really slow left-hander, Valentino was late on the brakes, on the inside, and squeezed round, lightly touching Sete's bike alongside. The Spaniard ran out of track and was unable to react. On the podium second-placed Sete was clearly upset, dark in the face, and the crowd whistled loudly. But Valentino did not care. He had completed his mission — to 'destroy' his main rival.

Gibernau was never again able to reach the same heights. The championship became a walkover for Rossi as he dominated without problems. There were just a few moments of glory for the others: Nicky Hayden welcomed the United States Grand Prix back to the calendar by winning at Laguna Seca, Loris Capirossi

ABOVE Marco Melandri finished the 2005 season in great style with wins in Turkey and Valencia.

RIGHT Nicky Hayden celebrates his first MotoGP win, in his home Grand Prix at Laguna Seca in 2005. Fellow American Colin Edwards (left) was second and Valentino Rossi third.

had two victories on the Ducati, and Marco Melandri, Gibernau's team-mate, closed the season by winning in Istanbul and Valencia, ending the year as championship runner-up.

In 2006 the perfect machine broke down from one day to the next. Yamaha and Rossi had to manage the unexpected. Technical problems, tyre problems, and also moments of bad karma… beginning with the first race at Jerez. At the start in Spain, Toni Elías put Valentino on the ground and victory went to Capirossi. This immediately showed the Ducati's potential, the Italian factory looking ready to win the championship. However, Catalunya cost Ducati any hope of the title: Gibernau, new to the Italian team, fell at the first corner, bringing down with him team-mates Melandri and Capirossi, both of whom sustained fractures and had to miss races. It was a disastrous moment for Ducati.

Rookie Dani Pedrosa, the double 250cc champion, finished second at Jerez on the HRC Honda. He quickly emerged as an unexpected title contender and at the fourth round, in China, celebrated his first win. His first year was supposed to be one of learning and of

ABOVE In 2006 Shinya Nakano brought Kawasaki its best MotoGP finish with second place at Assen.

BELOW Kenny Roberts Jr put the KR211V of his father's team on the podium at Estoril in 2006.

ABOVE Nicky Hayden leads team-mate Dani Pedrosa at the penultimate MotoGP round of 2006 in Portugal — a couple of laps later they tangled and crashed.

RIGHT Nicky Hayden's third place at the final MotoGP round of 2006 was enough for him to clinch the world title.

building experience and confidence ahead of a true title challenge in 2007, when the nimble 'super 250' 800cc machines were expected to better suit his style and small size. Dani won again in dominant fashion at Donington Park, but a struggle to 15th in tricky conditions at Phillip Island mathematically ended his impressive quest to be the first rookie to win the premier-class crown since Kenny Roberts Sr in 1978.

Meanwhile, Nicky Hayden, having won in the Netherlands and the USA, had the championship in his grasp, but in Portugal, the penultimate race, the unexpected happened: Pedrosa crashed and brought down his American team-mate. That meant that Rossi, second to Toni Elías in Portugal, went to the final round at Valencia back in the lead of the championship.

Hayden was ready for one last attack, trying to reverse their positions. At the start, Rossi was slower than the others, losing position and clearly in trouble. Eventually he crashed — the championship had slipped through his fingers! Troy Bayliss, World Superbike Champion and replacement for the injured Gibernau, won the race in front of Capirossi. Hayden finished third — and became World Champion.

LEFT World Superbike Champion Troy Bayliss took his only Grand Prix win for Ducati in that final 2006 round in Valencia.

LEFT The 2006 World Champion Nicky Hayden celebrates after the Valencia race.

CHAPTER 8
2007–2011
SIZE MAKES NO DIFFERENCE

BY JULIAN RYDER

OPPOSITE The magnificent Casey Stoner brought Ducati its first premier-class title and the first of the new 800cc era.

BELOW The story of the 2007 season: Casey Stoner leads Valentino Rossi's Yamaha and Dani Pedrosa's Honda.

The five years of MotoGP's 800cc formula were topped and tailed by Casey Stoner. He won the first year on Ducati and the final year on Honda and in between Yamaha dominated with first Valentino Rossi and then Jorge Lorenzo.

After the first five years of MotoGP ran to a 990cc limit, engine capacity and fuel load were reduced to try to keep lap times and top speeds in check. It did not quite work out that way as the engineers developed their second-generation MotoGP machines into 'super 250s' with high corner speeds and massively sophisticated electronics.

When a new formula comes in, it is not uncommon for one factory to hit the centre of the target and this,

as demonstrated in 2002, is usually Honda. To the shock of nearly everyone, the world's largest motorcycle manufacturer did not start the 800cc era as winners, and in fact it took ten races before Dani Pedrosa won for Honda in Germany, and then there was a further wait until the last race of the year for a second victory.

What actually happened was a shock. It was defined on the very first lap of the season in Qatar when Stoner drove his Ducati past Rossi's Yamaha on the front straight. He did not even have to use the slipstream and was well in front by the time he crossed the start/finish line. What had happened?

Honda built a small, nimble motorcycle but Ducati did what it always does and strived for as much power

ABOVE Dani Pedrosa won twice in 2007 to finish runner-up in the MotoGP World Championship.

RIGHT Laguna Seca's 2007 programme cover featured America's reigning World Champion.

FAR RIGHT Chris Vermeulen scored his only Grand Prix win and Suzuki's first for six years at the 2007 French Grand Prix.

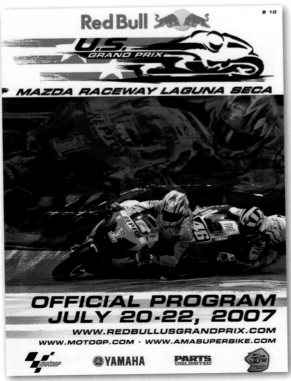

as possible and then used advanced electronics to tame it. And then there was the small matter of the rider. At the time, it was widely assumed that the 800cc Ducati gave its riders a massive advantage. This view conveniently overlooked that fact that the other three Ducati men proved unable to muster Stoner's points tally between them.

We did not really understand, but we were watching one of the very best there has ever been. Stoner was never out of the points, won ten races, and was off the rostrum only four times. We now know the bike was peaky and difficult to ride, and that Ducati would spend much of the rest of the 800cc era trying to find someone else who could ride it as it needed to be ridden, which was very hard indeed. Perspective now tells us that in 2007 we saw a genius at work.

The second year of the 800s was much less clear cut. Three different makes of motorcycle won the first three races and four different riders led the championship at some point in the season. Rossi, now with Bridgestone tyres on his Yamaha rather than Michelins, started the season with a lowly fifth place but thereafter he was on the podium every time bar one. Three wins in a row in

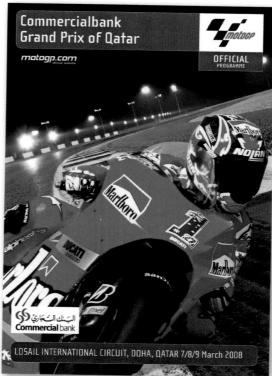

ABOVE Nicky Hayden and Dani Pedrosa lead the way at Jerez in 2008. Pedrosa won the race to take the championship lead.

LEFT The 2008 season kicked off in Qatar under the Losail International circuit's floodlights for the first motorcycle Grand Prix to be held in darkness.

ABOVE Jorge Lorenzo leads his Yamaha team-mate at Estoril in 2008.

OPPOSITE Double 250cc World Champion Jorge Lorenzo celebrates his first MotoGP victory at the 2008 Portuguese Grand Prix.

China, France and Italy put him at the top of the table with Stoner back in fourth.

By now, Rossi was more worried about his young new team-mate, Jorge Lorenzo, who had taken pole position for the first three races and won the third with the fastest lap to go top of the championship. Some mighty crashes took the stuffing out of Jorge's challenge but he recovered confidence in the second half of the year to finish fourth, at the time the best end-of-season result for a rookie in MotoGP.

Stoner did not look like he could mount a championship defence until after the Catalunya test, when Ducati sorted out its overly aggressive engine. Casey now embarked on a rampage of six consecutive poles, five fastest laps and three wins in a row — Britain, the Netherlands and Germany. The race at the Sachsenring saw the end of Pedrosa's challenge as he crashed while leading the wet race by over six seconds. Valentino now only had 20 points between himself and Stoner as opposed to the gap of 50 after Catalunya, and he described trying to beat Casey as 'like racing a UFO'.

The season turned on an incident in the very next race, Laguna Seca, just a week later. Rossi gave a masterclass in keeping a quicker bike behind you on a tight and twisty track. He never let Stoner lead onto the front straight because he knew that if he did the Ducati's speed would pull too big a gap down that straight for him to recover in the rest of the lap. So there was one audacious repass round the outside at Turn 4 and then there was that moment at The Corkscrew. Stoner led down the hill only for Rossi to cut inside, going off-track in the process. It turned out to be the decisive move of the season and the indelible image of the year. Stoner left America nursing a grudge and crashed in the next two races. Rossi went on to win the title with three races to spare and pass Giacomo Agostini's record of 68 wins in the top class.

That was Valentino's eighth world title and his sixth in the top class, and came in advance of yet another seismic shift in the technical regulations for 2009.

Stoner's runaway success in 2007 was not only a triumph for Ducati, but it was also the year that Bridgestone won its first premier-class title, having entered MotoGP at the start of the new four-stroke era in 2002. After initial teething problems, Bridgestone

ABOVE The clash of the 2008 season — Valentino Rossi versus Casey Stoner at Laguna Seca.

quickly established itself as a world leader in tyre development and, by 2008, it had taken over from Michelin as the preferred tyre choice of the top riders and factories.

It was during 2008 that the prospect of adopting a single tyre supplier gathered serious momentum. Concerns about the high corner speeds of the new-generation 800cc machines had been expressed and a switch to a single-tyre rule was considered one option to improve safety. Negotiations were protracted and Dorna CEO Carmelo Ezpeleta was in favour of retaining competition if Michelin could secure a deal to have eight bikes on the grid for the 2009 season.

Michelin found an unlikely ally in Ducati. Impressed by Bridgestone's improved performances during 2004, Ducati had gambled on a switch to Bridgestone for the 2005 season, a decision fully vindicated by Stoner's dominance two years later. Ducati was eager to see tyre competition remain and was willing to put its five entries for 2009 on Michelin rubber. However, Michelin was unable to convince any other manufacturer to take its tyres for 2009, so, after round-the-clock negotiations during the 2008 Japanese Grand Prix at Twin-Ring

Motegi, Ezpeleta confirmed that the single-tyre rule would be implemented.

With the entire field competing on Bridgestone rubber in 2009, it was Rossi who prevailed again, making it nine titles in all classes in a season in which he scored his 100th GP win and closed to within 20 of Ago's all-time record of 122 GP victories. Not bad for a 30-year-old made to work harder than ever by a trio of younger rivals — Lorenzo, Pedrosa and Stoner. Yes, Valentino won six races, but he said it was his toughest season. How hard was he having to ride? He crashed in three races, failed to win any of the last four races of the year, and his seven-race winning streak at Mugello came to an end.

There was also the matter of a team-mate who refused to be intimidated and was willing to go handlebar to handlebar with him. Lorenzo and Rossi fought out fierce duels at Catalunya, Sachsenring, Brno and Indianapolis. The Catalunya race was the highlight and provided another of those enduring images thanks to the best last lap of recent times. Lorenzo took the lead with a classic outbraking move at Turn 1, Rossi counter-attacked at every opportunity, but it looked

as if the young pretender would hold on — until the last corner. Into this fearsome downhill right-hander usually taken in third gear, Valentino somehow made a clean inside move and held onto the line. The great American champion Kevin Schwantz made an astute comment: 'That was about more than five points.' He was right: it was about Rossi asserting his authority over what he called 'the young sharks', and especially over Lorenzo. As for Jorge, he won four races and led the championship, not bad for a 22-year-old in his second MotoGP season.

Lorenzo ratcheted up the pressure on his team-mate in 2010. While Valentino Rossi did win the first race of the year, Jorge won the next two handily. That put Valentino in the unusual position of going to his home race as the one under pressure, nine points behind Lorenzo. That pressure duly got to Valentino in Free Practice: he slowed to let a follower come past then gassed it up into the Biondetti chicane and highsided himself. The impact broke his tibia and fibula, the first serious injury of Valentino's career. It is tempting to assume the injury was the pivotal moment of the year, but with hindsight it was the seemingly trivial

OFFICIAL PROGRAMME
motogp.com *official website*

Shell Advance Malaysian Motorcycle Grand Prix

24-25 October 2009 RM10

sepangcircuit.com

ADVANCE

ABOVE Jorge Lorenzo and Valentino Rossi slog it out with Casey Stoner at Barcelona in 2009.

LEFT Ducati won the 2009 Malaysian race but but with Casey Stoner rather than front-page star Nicky Hayden.

ABOVE Valentino Rossi crashing in front of eventual winner Andrea Dovizioso in the 2009 British Grand Prix at Donington Park.

RIGHT Andrea Dovizioso grabbed his first MotoGP win in difficult conditions at the 2009 British Grand Prix held at Donington Park for the last time.

tweaked shoulder he suffered in a motocross accident before Jerez that really made his life difficult. Jorge, meanwhile, had developed a robot-like efficiency. He started on the front row at every race except Japan and only finished off the rostrum twice. His first non-rostrum finish was at the 13th race of the year. He simply did not make any mistakes, and his pace forced the competition into their own mistakes.

Every time it looked like the pressure was getting to Lorenzo, on the grid at Brno, after the race in Motegi, he swiftly regained control. Rossi only missed four races while recovering from injury and his return was spectacular — and accompanied by a resumption of the mind games. Stoner was the target in Germany, Lorenzo in Japan, and there could not have been a more theatrical gesture than throwing his crutches to the crowd under the podium at Laguna Seca. Valentino only won one more race, a stormer in Malaysia, thus neatly distracting from Lorenzo clinching the title, his first.

It is easy to forget that Jorge started the year with the legacy of a nasty hand injury; he could not even shake hands at Qatar but managed a late charge to second place. In Jerez he banged fairings with Pedrosa in a fabulous last-lap duel and at Silverstone he ran away to lead every lap and win by a distance, the start of three wins in a row in which he was headed for just one lap. The winning margins were 6.7, 2.9 and 4.8 seconds. In all he won nine races but there was also a growing maturity about his public pronouncements.

LEFT Motorland Aragón in Spain joined the MotoGP schedule in 2010.

He grew up in public in the paddock and changed in front of us from, frankly, a brat into a very impressive champion who copes effortlessly with the responsibility of speaking for the sport.

Talking of change, 2010 marked a new chapter in the history of the intermediate World Championship.

BELOW Former bitter 250cc rivals Jorge Lorenzo and Dani Pedrosa fight it out at Jerez in 2010.

ABOVE Jorge Lorenzo heads the packed field at Assen in 2010. He won the race en route to his first MotoGP title.

BELOW Forget the crutches — Valentino Rossi still finished on the podium at Laguna Seca in 2010.

The 250cc two-stroke machine had been a mainstay of World Championship racing since its inception back in 1949. While many mourned the loss of the sublime 250s, the move to make the paddock exclusively four-stroke continued at an unrelenting pace when the new Moto2 category was introduced for 2010.

Two-stroke 250s were works of art, but the field had become more about quantity than quality. Spiralling costs and a lack of competition prompted Dorna to take decisive action and the result was a more affordable class that would promote increased competition at a cheaper price. All Moto2 bikes ran a mandatory Honda 600cc engine, which was a lightly tuned version of its standard CBR600RR production motor capable of producing close to 125bhp. Controlled tyres and electronics kept a lid on costs but the main technical intrigue would come from the fact that a prototype chassis was permitted.

Toni Elías has the distinction of winning the first Moto2 title in 2010, while Marc Márquez, Pol Espargaro, Tito Rabat and Johann Zarco all went on to race in the MotoGP World Championship after graduating from Moto2 as World Champion.

Meanwhile, as Jorge cruised to his first MotoGP
title in 2010, the paddock was alive with rumours of
one of the biggest moves in bike racing history. Would
Valentino really leave Yamaha and go to under-achievers
Ducati? And would it be an Italian dream team — or a
national disaster?

Ducati had to make room for Rossi on the factory
team by letting Casey Stoner head off to Honda. On
the grounds that no other rider had managed to win
on a Ducati since 2007, the pressure was on Rossi and
his team to prove their genius and perform one more
miracle to add to the list. Honda, meanwhile, had so far
failed to win a championship under the 800cc formula,
and this was their last chance.

Then there was Jorge Lorenzo, ready to put up a
strong defence of his title but undone by two small
errors. He crashed in monsoon conditions at Silverstone,
which lost him the championship lead, and he was
taken out on the first lap at the next race, Assen, but
remounted to finish sixth. However, he could never claw
back the advantage that Casey Stoner on the much-
improved Honda opened up.

Stoner finished on the rostrum at every race except

ABOVE Casey Stoner arrived from Ducati to win first time out on the factory Honda at Qatar in 2011.

LEFT Casey Stoner and HRC Vice-President Shuhei Nakamoto celebrate the 2011 world title.

Jerez, where he was torpedoed by Rossi, and failed to start from the front row only once. Ten race wins made him only the fifth man to win the title on different makes of motorcycle, alongside Geoff Duke, Giacomo Agostini, Eddie Lawson and Valentino Rossi.

The last named in that list had a horrible year, more Italian nightmare than dream team. But that paled into insignificance beside the loss of MotoGP's rising star Marco Simoncelli. The fans' favourite lost his life on the second lap of the Malaysian GP when he fell and was hit by following bikes. This came just a week after the best race of his MotoGP career, second to Stoner in Australia. He had got over his crashing tendency and surely would have won a race soon. The championship? We will never know.

The 800cc era was dominated by Rossi and Stoner who won, respectively, 37.5 per cent and 24 per cent of the 88 races. The only others to win more than one race were Lorenzo and Pedrosa. The equivalent figures for podiums are 66 per cent and 54.5 per cent — both staggering numbers. The dominant bike was the Yamaha M-1 with 39 wins, just over 44 per cent.

By the end of their five-year life, the 800s were lapping most tracks as quickly as the 990s they replaced despite being slightly slower in a straight line. MotoGP decided it was time to go back to litre bikes in an attempt to reduce corner speeds. If the 800s demonstrated one thing, it is that you can do what you like with the regulations, but fast guys will always be fast.

ABOVE Marco Simoncelli savours his second place in the 2011 Australian Grand Prix — the best result of his MotoGP career.

OPPOSITE Grand Prix motorcycle racing suffered the loss of a real legend when Marco Simoncelli lost his life at Sepang in 2011.

RIGHT All gloom and doom for Valentino Rossi and Ducati in 2011.

CHAPTER 9
2012–2016
GOLDEN AGE
BY MATT BIRT

The latest chapter in Dorna's proud 25-year history of running the MotoGP World Championship is one that will undoubtedly be fondly remembered as a golden age for the sport.

Fierce and bitter rivalries both old and new contributed to some of the closest and most combative racing ever witnessed. There was genuine competition between multiple manufacturers for the first time in a generation. And it was all thanks to a brave new technical revolution. Add in a rapidly expanding global TV audience and record live crowds, and interest in MotoGP was never higher or the future more healthy.

The chapter started in 2012 in entirely predictable fashion, with Jorge Lorenzo and reigning World Champion Casey Stoner sharing the first three victories. Stoner's successes in Jerez and Estoril, however, came against a blizzard of rumours that he was ready to drop a bombshell and retire at the age of 27. For a racer to walk away from the sport when seemingly at the peak of his powers was almost unheard of. And when the outspoken Australian vehemently rebuked rumours of his premature departure after victory in Estoril, it seemed a case of case closed. So there was an overpowering sense of astonishment, respect and bewilderment when Stoner confirmed during an emotionally charged pre-event press conference in Le Mans that 2012 would be his farewell.

Back on the track, Stoner's win in the historic Dutch TT left him locked on 140 points with Lorenzo, whose purple patch of three successive victories was ended when Álvaro Bautista torpedoed him out of contention on the first lap at Assen. It was the last lap in Germany just two weeks later when the pendulum swung back in favour of Lorenzo after Stoner crashed his Repsol Honda just two corners from the chequered flag while lining up a last-gasp attack on team-mate Dani Pedrosa.

Lorenzo and Stoner then exchanged wins at Mugello and Laguna Seca before the Aussie's hopes of a valedictory success in his swansong season were ended by a vicious qualifying crash at the Indianapolis Motor Speedway. Stoner suffered serious ligament damage in his right ankle but heroically raced to fourth place just 24 hours later.

Stoner fully intended to ride through the pain barrier again in Brno but additional medical checks showed the injury was of such severity that unless he underwent immediate surgery he risked potentially life-changing damage. He was forced to take three races off, which was terminal to his title hopes, although he did return in time to power to an unprecedented sixth straight win at Phillip Island.

His last act was a podium in treacherous conditions

RIGHT Casey Stoner and Dani Pedrosa delivered a one-two for Honda at Assen in 2012.

LEFT Jorge Lorenzo
secured his second
MotoGP crown in 2012.

in Valencia ahead of a departure that stirred up contrasting emotions. There was the gratitude at being present to marvel at the skills of one of the fastest riders in history. But there was more than a tinge of regret that we would no longer see him ride in anger again, even though speculation has persisted ever since of an unlikely comeback.

Stoner's injury problems meant the title chase became a two-horse race between Lorenzo and Pedrosa. Five wins in six races kept Pedrosa pressuring Lorenzo, but a second-lap crash in Australia while leading dealt a terminal blow to his prospects and Lorenzo secured his second premier-class crown with his eighth second place in 10 races.

It was in 2012 that the MotoGP World Championship finally completed its journey to becoming an exclusively four-stroke arena. MotoGP had gone entirely four-stroke in 2003 after a transition season in 2002. The 250cc two-strokes were banished to the history books at the end of 2009, when the 600cc four-stroke Moto2 category arrived. The total demise of the two-stroke era was on the cards midway through 2010, when the UK-based *Motor Cycle News* broke the story

GRAN PREMIO **GENERALI**
GENERALI DE LA
COMUNITAT
VALENCIANA
VALENCIA 09-11/11/2012
PROGRAMA OFICIAL €8

LEFT Valencia ended a
tough 2012 season for
Valentino Rossi, who took
just two podium finishes.

ABOVE Andrea Dovizioso brought the Tech3 Yamaha team fourth place in the 2012 World Championship.

RIGHT German Sandro Cortese won the very first Moto3 World Championship in 2012.

in June that year that a new class called Moto3 would replace the 125cc World Championship.

The success of the inaugural Moto2 series had convinced Dorna of the viability and potential success of Moto3. Moto2 had attracted fresh sponsorship investment and the increased exposure meant several 125 teams were eager to move. At the same time, the performance gap between the top 125cc two-strokes and the rest of the field was becoming alarmingly large. A shake-up of the entry-level class would inject fresh life into it and deliver a bigger entry list and lower costs.

The new Moto3 class would feature a 250cc single-cylinder four-stroke engine but, unlike Moto2, a single manufacturer would not supply the engine. Moto3 has rightly been hailed an overwhelming success, with Honda, KTM and Indian marque Mahindra all victorious.

Germany's Sandro Cortese wrote his name in the record books by becoming the first Moto3 World Champion. And the series has since proved to be an excellent breeding ground for young talent, with Maverick Viñales, Jack Miller, Alex Rins and Jonas Folger all serving their apprenticeship in Moto3 before moving to the ranks of MotoGP.

The 250cc single-cylinder four-stroke format has also been adopted in a wide-ranging series of international Dorna-backed feeder classes like the FIM CEV Repsol Junior World Championship, Idemitsu Asia Talent Cup and Red Bull Rookies MotoGP Cup, which have been specifically created to unearth and nurture future generations of Grand Prix star talent.

A big question going into 2013 would be how MotoGP would cope without a star like Stoner? Well, in truth his absence was barely noticeable. MotoGP had been so dominated by Rossi, Stoner, Lorenzo and Pedrosa that they were affectionately referred to as 'aliens'. It was a phrase coined to emphasise the elite quartet's superiority and was meant to reflect their riding as being out of this world and not human.

Just as one of the aliens retired, another materialised immediately. Marc Márquez had harvested a reputation for being a ruthless and aggressive competitor when blazing a trail through the 125cc and Moto2 categories, and that made him a heaven-sent replacement for Stoner at HRC. After Doohan, Crivillé, Rossi, Hayden and Stoner, Márquez instantly set about continuing the

ABOVE Marc Márquez leads team-mate Dani Pedrosa at Austin in 2013 on the way to his first MotoGP win.

LEFT Marc Márquez featured on the programme cover for the 2013 Spanish Grand Prix — only his third MotoGP race.

ABOVE Valentino Rossi battling with Dani Pedrosa at Assen in 2013 on the way to his first win since Malaysia three years earlier.

BELOW Rossi's one race win of 2013 meant a lot after his lean spell but team-mate Jorge Lorenzo won eight that year.

Repsol Honda dynasty with a series of astounding performances.

Márquez valiantly jousted with Rossi for second place in the season's opening encounter in Qatar before becoming the youngest rider in history to win in the premier class in Austin in only his second race. The established elite then got full warning that the young Spaniard cared little for reputations with a merciless barge past Lorenzo at the final corner in Jerez, a tactic that instantly soured relations between the pair. Márquez then had the fastest crash ever recorded in Grand Prix history with a terrifying front-wheel lock-up at close to 330km/h when braking at the end of Mugello's fearsome start/finish straight during practice.

The turning point of the campaign came around the tight and twisty curves of Germany's Sachsenring. Heading to Germany, Márquez was only third in the rankings and trailed series leader Pedrosa by 23 points and Lorenzo by 14 points. Pedrosa's challenge was to unravel yet again in the cruellest and most heart-wrenching way. He suffered a partial fracture of his left collarbone in a Saturday morning practice tumble but the injury was not deemed serious enough to rule him

out of the race. The subsequent trauma, however, left him suffering from abnormally low blood pressure and he was declared unfit.

By that stage of proceedings, Lorenzo was already a confirmed absentee. Lorenzo's pain threshold seemed to know no bounds at the previous round in Assen when he raced to a superhuman fifth place less than 48 hours after snapping his left collarbone in two in a wet second-practice crash. When over-confidence crept in during Sachsenring's second practice and Lorenzo was launched into orbit again, there were to be no more heroics. The titanium plate inserted with 10 screws from the Assen crash was bent and the collarbone rebroken.

Márquez pounced on his compatriot's misfortune to go on a decisive four-race winning streak, although his relentless charge towards history was not without incident and controversy. He dislocated his left shoulder in a warm-up crash at Silverstone before suffering a last-corner defeat to Lorenzo. His aggressive tactics were again under the microscope after he won at Motorland Aragón. A split-second moment of contact between Márquez and Pedrosa had somehow cut a rear-wheel speed sensor on Dani's machine. With his

traction-control system instantly immobilised, Pedrosa was fired into the air and with it his fading title hopes were once again extinguished.

With a 43-point advantage and just three races remaining, Márquez seemed set to cruise to the honour of being the first rookie to win the premier-class title since American legend Kenny Roberts did so in 1978. But he almost hit the self-destruct button with the winning post in sight.

Safety concerns over tyre endurance on a new surface at Phillip Island meant a mandatory pit stop was enforced to change to fresh Bridgestone rubber after nine or 10 laps. Inexplicably, Márquez and his crew made a shocking howler and miscalculated exactly when the window to pit was open. He was subsequently black-flagged and disqualified. Wins in Australia and Japan from Lorenzo narrowed the lead down to 13 points but a relatively trouble-free ride to third behind Lorenzo and Pedrosa in Valencia gave Márquez the prize.

A footnote to 2013 was the return to Yamaha of prodigal son Valentino Rossi after a disastrous two-year stint at Ducati. He spent much of the year trying to

ABOVE Marc Márquez's third place at the last round of 2013 gave him the MotoGP world title in his début season.

ABOVE Ten in a row for Marc Márquez in 2014 as he crosses the line at the famed Indianapolis Motor Speedway in America.

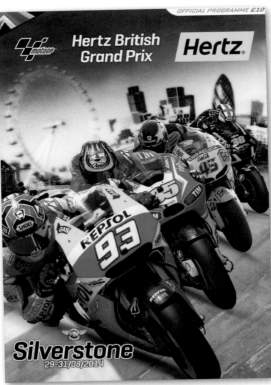

RIGHT Since 2010 Silverstone has become the established home of the British Grand Prix.

rediscover the razor-sharp edge required to cope with the cut-throat nature of racing at the front in MotoGP and the highlight was a solitary win in Assen.

The breathtaking brilliance of Márquez and Rossi's return to winning ways made 2013 feel like a vintage year. Although Rossi's star may have waned while in the doldrums at Ducati, the arrival of Márquez as a new king still could not dethrone Rossi from his undisputed position as poster boy for the World Championship.

If Márquez had left it late to triumph in 2013, then his second season in MotoGP was one of utter dominance and he successfully defended the title in much more convincing and emphatic fashion. He was victorious in the first 10 races and there was a genuine sense that he could go undefeated and complete the perfect season. His remarkable winning streak was finally ended when Pedrosa prevailed in Brno but he still ended the season with a record 13 wins and a commanding advantage of 67 points.

The demolition might have been more devastating had Marc not crashed while battling Rossi for the lead in Misano. He lapsed when trying to lead on slicks in a

ABOVE Valentino Rossi sent the home crowd wild with his victory at Misano in 2014.

LEFT Dani Pedrosa kept up Honda's clean sweep of 2014 by beating Jorge Lorenzo in the Czech Republic Grand Prix.

downpour at Motorland Aragón and another win went begging at Phillip Island when he crashed with a lead of over four seconds.

Márquez's rampant run did not make 2014 feel like the dull and sterile affairs that one-man exhibitions usually bring. Rossi should take the credit for that as he delivered yet more age-defying performances with wins at Misano and Phillip Island, along with 10 other podiums.

We wondered how MotoGP could make us any more euphoric and then came a truly unforgettable 2015.

A classic season started with an evergreen Rossi rolling back the years again with victories in two of the first three races that hinted at his strongest title challenge since his last success back in 2009. An engrossing tussle between Rossi and Márquez in Argentina ended in elation for the Italian and deflation for Márquez. Márquez crashed after making contact with Rossi's Yamaha YZR-M1 and he was to get his nose bloodied again in Assen, where Rossi won a memorable last-corner duel to bring an abrupt end to the best purple patch of Lorenzo's career that stretched over four successive wins. At the time, there was no inclination that the events that unfolded in Argentina and Assen were ultimately to have colossal consequences at the conclusion of a World Championship that for 16 out of 18 races was a masterpiece.

With three races remaining when the paddock headed south to Phillip Island, Rossi and Lorenzo were split by just 18 points, with Rossi a firm favourite to capture a 10th title that nobody could deny would have been universally popular.

In Australia Rossi, Lorenzo, Márquez and Ducati's Andrea Iannone treated fans to a spectacle so intense and dramatic that it was instantly branded 'The Race of the Decade'. There were 52 overtakes between the quartet and everybody was ready to wax lyrical about that race for years to come… except for Rossi and those closest to him who cried foul and conspiracy.

While the world reflected on an instant classic on that Sunday in Australia, behind the scenes Rossi was deeply suspicious that a dark force had been at work to help manipulate the outcome against him. That dark force was Márquez.

Márquez had produced a scintillating final lap in Australia to win ahead of Lorenzo, with Rossi relegated to fourth after losing out to Iannone. Just four days later during a highly charged pre-event press conference for the Sepang race in Malaysia, Rossi sent shockwaves around the world when he claimed Márquez had deliberately tried to manipulate the result to enhance Lorenzo's title prospects to the detriment of his own. Rossi was so aggrieved that in a post-conference media scrum with Italian journalists he produced a print-out of the lap times from Phillip Island to back up his argument with hard evidence.

Márquez and Rossi once enjoyed a convivial rapport that back in 2013 bore all the hallmarks of a master-and-apprentice relationship. By 2015 Márquez had served his time and Rossi was no longer the all-

BELOW The fuse was already lit when Valentino Rossi and Marc Márquez clashed at Assen's final corner in 2015.

ABOVE Even a seagull cannot halt the progress of Andrea Iannone as he leads the snarling pack down Lukey Heights at Phillip Island in that epic 2015 encounter.

LEFT The infamous press conference at Sepang in 2015 — Jorge Lorenzo (left) looks on as Valentino Rossi and Marc Márquez exchange views.

ABOVE The most talked-about race of the decade — Marc Márquez leads the way from Valentino Rossi in the 2015 Malaysian Grand Prix.

PROGRAMA OFICIAL 10€

movistar

Gran Premio Movistar de Aragón

25-26-27 SEPTIEMBRE 2015

RIGHT Jorge Lorenzo won in Aragón to push on with his MotoGP title bid.

conquering master of ceremonies that he had been earlier in his distinguished career. The breakdown in their relationship can be traced back to those incidents in Argentina and Holland: Rossi, adamant that Márquez wanted to exact some sort of revenge for those defeats, viewed the Phillip Island classic as the moment when his Spanish foe opted to retaliate.

A full-blown war of words sent their relationship into meltdown in Sepang and the animosity spilled off the home pages and front pages onto the track.

Pedrosa's stunning victory in Sepang was completely forgotten. Earlier in the race, Rossi and Márquez engaged in a confrontation that was about far more than World Championship points. The heated exchange lasted for just seven laps but its controversial climax became one of the biggest talking points in MotoGP history. Contact between the pair before the hard acceleration point onto the long back straight resulted in Márquez crashing and Rossi's title aspirations facing dire consequences. Yet more mud-slinging followed, with Rossi accusing Márquez of blatantly disrupting his race.

Rossi came to Valencia in the ascendancy over

Lorenzo by just seven points, but he paid a hefty price for his involvement in the Márquez mêlée in Malaysia. Race Direction hit Rossi with three penalty points and, added to the one he received for impeding Lorenzo on a hot lap in qualifying at Misano in September, it meant that he would have to start from the back of the grid for the title decider. Rossi personally appealed his penalty to the Court of Arbitration for Sport but his plea to get the sanction overturned failed.

The Rossi/Márquez war that raged in Australia and Malaysia inevitably provoked a media frenzy. Determined to try to defuse the situation, Dorna decided to take the unprecedented step of cancelling the pre-event press conference in Valencia. Instead, Dorna CEO Carmelo Ezpeleta and FIM President Vito Ippolito chaired a meeting between them and the MotoGP grid to try to further calm stormy waters.

The final showdown brought yet more controversy. A gallant charge through to fourth place was inconsequential for Rossi, for Lorenzo's victory condemned him to a second premier-class title defeat in Valencia. In a nail-biting final few laps, Lorenzo came under immense pressure from Márquez, but

ABOVE Jorge Lorenzo won at the final round in 2015 at Valencia to seal his fifth world title.

BELOW The real Jorge Lorenzo with four clones representing his status as a five-time World Champion.

ABOVE Marc Márquez was often in the Yamaha sandwich of Jorge Lorenzo and Valentino Rossi during 2016.

RIGHT Jerez in Spain staged the first European Grand Prix of the incredible 2016 season.

Marc never attacked in the face of Jorge's surgeon-like precision. Had Márquez and Pedrosa, who was also in contention, overtaken Lorenzo, then Rossi would have been crowned World Champion. Rossi was left with such a bitter taste in his mouth that he renewed his verbal assault on Márquez by accusing him of protecting Lorenzo to ensure his compatriot won the title.

Once the dust had settled on a terrific yet turbulent 2015, the big question was how 2016 could even get close to matching that drama? Nobody, though, could have envisaged just how much excitement lay ahead.

The start of the 2016 season was anything but extraordinary. Márquez, Rossi and Lorenzo shared the opening seven victories between them and everything was running to a predictable script. The highlight of this part of the season was an epic last-lap showdown at Mugello between Lorenzo and Márquez, Jorge taking his third win by just 0.019 second (the seventh-closest finish in premier-class history) to lead the series by 10 points. But then Lorenzo's challenge faltered and he had to wait until the season finale in Valencia to win again.

From Assen onwards, 2016 was suddenly transformed into the craziest, most unpredictable and memorable season in the 68-year history of the World Championship.

The catalyst for records galore being broken and the history books being torn up almost on every lap was Jack Miller's measured ride to victory in the Dutch TT after Rossi had crashed out of a relatively comfortable lead.

Normal service seemed to have been resumed when Márquez won a flag-to-flag encounter in Germany with a ride of audacity and ambition that has become his trademark.

Ducati's six-year wait to end its long victory drought was ended by Andrea Iannone at the fearsomely fast Red Bull Ring in Austria. A last-minute decision to run the softest rear Michelin proved a tactical masterstroke by Iannone, who denied team-mate Andrea Dovizioso the kudos of returning Ducati to the top step of the podium.

More history was created just seven days later at Brno when Cal Crutchlow, inspired by a bold move to run Michelin's hard-compound rain tyres,

ABOVE Australian Jack Miller was a popular winner of the wet 2016 Dutch TT at Assen.

BELOW The magnificent Red Bull Ring in Austria joined the MotoGP calendar in 2016.

ABOVE & RIGHT Andrea
Iannone leads the way on
the factory Ducati at the
Red Bull Ring in 2016
and celebrates his first
MotoGP win.

became Britain's first premier class winner since Barry
Sheene triumphed at Anderstorp in Sweden way
back in 1981.

Rising star Maverick Viñales then handed Suzuki
its first victory since 2007 with a commanding win
at Silverstone before Dani Pedrosa continued the
astonishing sequence at the Misano World Circuit
Marco Simoncelli. It was another key tyre choice that
proved pivotal, with Pedrosa going against convention
by racing a soft front tyre to success.

A remarkable ninth different winner in a row did
not materialise at Motorland Aragón after Márquez
put on another exhibition. But a record-breaking ninth
different winner did emerge in Sepang when Andrea
Dovizioso won for the first time since the 2009 British
Grand Prix at Donington Park.

By that stage, Márquez was already a triple
MotoGP World Champion at the age of just 23. The
title in the craziest of crazy seasons was decided
in crazy fashion at the Twin-Ring Motegi in Japan.
Márquez arrived at Honda's home race knowing that
a highly improbable set of circumstances would need
to go his way to clinch a fifth World Championship

LEFT Cal Crutchlow became the first British premier-class winner for 35 long years with his MotoGP win at Brno in 2016.

BELOW LEFT Maverick Viñales celebrates his first MotoGP victory, at the 2016 British Grand Prix.

BELOW Rain-master Andrea Dovizioso fought through the spray in the 2016 Malaysian Grand Prix to bring Ducati its second win of the season.

ABOVE Marc Márquez leads his two biggest 2016 rivals at Motegi in Japan.

BELOW What a season — the nine separate 2016 MotoGP winners celebrate in Valencia.

OPPOSITE Marc Márquez secured his fifth world title with victory in the 2016 Japanese Grand Prix.

success. He needed to win in Japan for the first time in his premier-class career and then hope that Rossi did not finish higher than 15th and Lorenzo higher than fourth. Márquez kept his end of the bargain. When Rossi and Lorenzo both slid out of second place, what had seemed like mission impossible was accomplished.

The dramatic and implausible way in which Márquez wrapped up the title perfectly summed up a season that will live long in the memory for those privileged to be part of it and for those who witnessed it.

The year started with trepidation at the beginning of a bold new technical revolution, with Michelin taking over from Bridgestone as the exclusive tyre supplier and the introduction of controlled electronics across the board. These measures were intended to level the playing field and make it cheaper and easier for small manufacturers and independent teams to be competitive.

By the end of 2016, at the conclusion of the 25-year revolution, MotoGP was undoubtedly the greatest motorsport show on earth.

PART 3

BATTLES AND BATTLEGROUNDS
MEMORABLE MOMENTS AND PLACES

The four-way fight at Phillip Island in 2015 between Marc Márquez, Jorge Lorenzo,
Andrea Iannone and Valentino Rossi was instantly hailed as the 'Race of the Decade'.

CHAPTER 10
THE TOP-TEN BATTLES
BY MATT BIRT

1979
SILVERSTONE

This epic battle between Kenny Roberts and Barry Sheene, who engaged in one of the fiercest rivalries in history, is widely regarded as one of the greatest motorcycle Grands Prix of all time. The pair went head-to-head over 28 breathless laps during which they memorably exchanged hand gestures before American Roberts took the win by just 0.03 second.

It became the defining race of their intense rivalry, with Roberts famously saying years later that he only got out of bed to beat Sheene. Despite their bitter rivalry, they went on to become close friends in retirement until Sheene's death in 2003.

1991
HOCKENHEIM

The rivalry between Wayne Rainey and Kevin Schwantz was so antagonistic that it has gone down in MotoGP history as one of the most intense conflicts of all time, on and off track. Their duelling was typified by their famous last-lap fight for victory in a nail-biting German Grand Prix at Hockenheim in 1991.

Hockenheim was dauntingly fast and a track where fortune favoured the brave. Rainey slipstreamed Schwantz into the lead on the final lap, only seconds later to see the tenacious Texan produce an outrageously courageous and daring overtake. As the pair entered the stadium section, Schwantz's Suzuku RGV500 was sideways at 290km/h when he lunged inside Rainey. There was no time for the Californian to retaliate and Schwantz won by just 0.016 second.

1996
BRNO

The tension between Álex Crivillé and Mick Doohan had been simmering throughout 1996 after the Spaniard's last-corner crash while they jostled for the win in Jerez.

Revenge was sweet for Crivillé in Brno when he shadowed Doohan for the entire 22-lap race before snatching a stunning last-gasp win after the Australian led exiting the final turn. Crivillé won a thriller by just 0.002 second in what remains the second closest finish in Grand Prix history.

2001
PHILLIP ISLAND

The 2001 Australian Grand Prix at Phillip Island was the day on which Valentino Rossi claimed his first title in the premier class, but the manner in which he achieved the feat is sometimes forgotten. He defeated Max Biaggi by just 0.013 second after an incredible last-lap fight. In the long and acrimonious feud between these two Italian riders, this tussle was one of the most intense. The race itself was unforgettable, with just 2.8 seconds covering the top nine.

2004
WELKOM

It may not have been the closest victory in Grand Prix history, but the excitement it delivered and the momentous shift in power it triggered makes Valentino Rossi's emotional début win for Yamaha in South Africa a milestone clash. Banned from testing for Yamaha until just three months before the season opener after his move from Honda, Rossi defied the odds to defeat HRC and Max Biaggi at the end of a titanic duel over 28 laps. The images of him kissing his famous number 46 and sitting trackside in tears and being mentally and physically drained are forever etched in people's memories. Rossi's success was the catalyst for Yamaha to embark on the most golden era in its history.

2005
JEREZ

Valentino Rossi and Sete Gibernau were once close pals in the paddock, but by 2005 their relationship had gone through a very public and rancorous meltdown. It was at Jerez's final corner, when Gibernau was on the brink of a famous home win, that things came to a head.

Ruthless Rossi lunged up the inside at the final turn and the contact pushed Gibernau into the gravel trap. You could cut the atmosphere in parc fermé with a knife as Gibernau could not conceal his disgust at Rossi's aggressive tactics.

2006
ESTORIL

The Portuguese Grand Prix in 2006 is frequently remembered for the infamous clash between Repsol Honda team-mates Dani Pedrosa and Nicky Hayden, which looked to have cost the American the chance of being crowned World Champion. But later in the same race, Toni Elías defeated Valentino Rossi by a whisker in one of the most tense and dramatic races of the four-stroke era. The Spaniard started 11th and was third at the beginning of the final lap behind Rossi and Kenny Roberts Jr. The American thought he had won the race having the led over the line on the penultimate lap, only to have miscalculated the number of laps completed. Elías beat Rossi by just 0.002 second and the magnitude of that victory only became evident two weeks later in Valencia when Rossi lost the crown to Hayden.

2008
LAGUNA SECA

This incredible California clash between Valentino Rossi and Casey Stoner is still regarded as one of the most ferocious and keenly contested battles of the modern era, even though they were split by 13 seconds at the chequered flag. Stoner was odds-on favourite to win after dominating practice and qualifying for Ducati, and Rossi even joked before the race that he would need a 30-second start to win.

For the first 24 laps, the action was non-stop and mesmerising, with the pair trading several daring overtakes. The most famous swoop was by Rossi at the spectacular Corkscrew section. But fans were denied a show-stopping finale when Stoner crashed at the final corner with eight laps to go.

2009
CATALUNYA

Just about every superlative in the dictionary has been used to describe the incredible last-corner victory by Valentino Rossi over Jorge Lorenzo at the Barcelona track in 2009. The last three laps of a truly pulsating 25-lap race were some of the most frenetic in living memory, with Rossi and Lorenzo trading constant overtakes.

Lorenzo thought he had done enough to win when he led going into the final corner, an advantage that usually means victory is secure. But an ingenious piece of improvisation from Rossi saw him conjure up a bold but brilliantly executed pass to strike a huge psychological blow against Lorenzo.

2016
MUGELLO

When Marc Márquez powered his Repsol Honda out of the final corner at Mugello ahead of Jorge Lorenzo, it looked a certainty he would take victory after Valentino Rossi was ruled out by a spectacular engine blow-up. But within inches of the finish line, Lorenzo used a perfect slipstream to pounce for the win by just 0.019 second.

It was the seventh closest finish in premier-class history and the second time Lorenzo had triumphed by less than 0.1 second against Márquez, the previous occasion having been at Silverstone in 2013 when a gap of just 0.081 second split them.

CHAPTER 11
THE TOP-TEN BATTLEGROUNDS
BY NICK HARRIS

STRUBBEN, ASSEN

For over 50 years, Strubben, at the Dutch circuit of Assen, was surely the most photographed corner in the world. This banked left-hander leading into the Veenslang was a photographer's and rider's dream. As always, the surface at Assen — the only circuit from the original 1949 calendar still being used today — provided plenty of grip and Strubben, with its banked profile, offered superb overtaking opportunities. The corner was first used in 1955 when the Assen circuit changed from its original road course and disappeared in 2006 when the track was modified. Its very mention conjures up memories of classic black-and-white photographs, as in this one of Mike Hailwood chasing Giacomo Agostini in 1965.

DEGNER CURVE, SUZUKA

This is a magnificent double right-hand bend approaching the underpass at the figure-of-eight Suzuka circuit in Japan. It was originally a fast right-hander that was changed to a double bend for safety reasons. In 1987 Grand Prix racing returned to the superb 5.807-kilometre Suzuka circuit and immediately the riders loved the Degner curve, named after Ernst Degner, who escaped from the old East Germany with two-stroke know-how from MZ that helped Suzuki to success in the 50cc World Championship — but Degner received severe burns in a crash in 1963 at the corner subsequently named in his honour. Grand Prix racing ceased at Suzuka in 2003 following the fatal crash of Japanese Honda rider Daijiro Kato.

WOODCOTE, SILVERSTONE

The high-speed right-hander that propelled riders into the start/finish straight at the fast and flat Silverstone circuit brought motorcycle racing to millions of British television viewers for the very first time in 1979. This was a bend of the seventies, frighteningly fast, with little run-off between the towering grandstands — and when Kenny Roberts and Barry Sheene arrived there approaching 200km/h on that fateful August afternoon the British viewing public were spellbound. For the previous 27 laps the duo had duelled tooth and nail before Woodcote would decide the winner. Roberts took the chequered flag just 0.03 second in front of Sheene, who had tried to ride round the outside of the American on the grass.

This classic encounter, also illustrated in the previous chapter, was so intense that in this photo of Sheene speeding through Woodcote his combatant is barely visible.

BALLAUGH BRIDGE, ISLE OF MAN

This hump-back bridge in the parish of Ballaugh on the A3 Castletown-to-Ramsey Road is not exactly a battleground but nonetheless it is an iconic section of the famous 60.721-kilometre mountain TT circuit on the Isle of Man that staged that very first World Championship race in 1949.

After 27 tortuous kilometres on the TT course, riders roar through the Alpine Cottage bends and down to Ballaugh, where they leap over the bridge, between its white railings, before accelerating away towards the super-fast Sulby Straight. This is a spot that sums up what the TT is all about. Our photo shows the scene in 1960 with John Surtees leaping high on his 350cc MV Agusta in the Junior TT.

EAU ROUGE, SPA-FRANCORCHAMPS

This high-speed section of the legendary Spa-Francorchamps circuit in Belgium is not a place for the faint-hearted. Riders blast downhill between the grandstands and old pit complex from La Source hairpin to be confronted by the flat-out left/right corner at the bottom of the hill, and then in a blink they are climbing steeply through an uphill right-hander towards a blind crest.

In 1977 Barry Sheene brought Suzuki success at Spa averaging a staggering 217.37km/h per hour for the ten laps round the 14.12-kilometre circuit. On my first visit to Spa, in 1974, at the end of the first lap Phil Read appeared at La Source with nobody else in sight, and the sight and sound of his magnificent MV Agusta disappearing over the rise after Eau Rouge remains a special memory. Two of the distant riders in this photo, taken in 1975, are Sheene and Read.

TURN 13, LORENZO CORNER, JEREZ

No other final corner in the 68-year history of World Championship racing has provided such drama. Turn 13 at the 4.423-kilometre Jerez circuit in southern Spain is top. This tight left-hander with the chequered flag in sight after a fast approach has witnessed the final seconds of some sensational battles.

One of the most notable, as pictured, occurred on the last lap in 1996 when Mick Doohan dived under crowd favourite Álex Crivillé, who tried to regain the advantage and highsided into the gravel trap, prompting emotional spectators to invade the track. Valentino Rossi and Sete Gibernau famously clashed at the same corner nine years later and Rossi has since been joined in the tradition by Marc Márquez and Jorge Lorenzo — whose name the corner now carries.

STONER, PHILLIP ISLAND

The problem with the magnificent Phillip Island in Australia is that it has so many great corners and three premier-class World Champions to name them after. The Gardner corner leads onto the start/finish straight and that is followed by the fast Doohan right-hander, and both are contenders for the circuit's best corner.

But for anybody who has watched Casey Stoner slide first the Ducati and then the Honda through the incredibly fast Turn Three, this has to be the winner. No wonder they named this corner after the six-time Phillip Island victor, having witnessed smoke pouring off the rear tyre at 200km/h with the magnificent Bass Strait providing the perfect ocean backdrop. Poetry in motion.

90-DEGREE, MOTEGI

If you had to name the most deceptive bend in MotoGP, this would be it.
The big gravel trap is the give-away because the 90-degree corner at Motegi
has caught out many a good rider. You come over the flat-out blind rise
on the back straight before the track suddenly drops away and there it is
looming up at you: a sharp 90-degree right-hander leading to the second
tunnel on the circuit.

It is a particularly exciting place for the smaller classes, as team-mates
Sandro Cortese and Danny Kent demonstrated with their mighty Moto3
coming together in 2012, as pictured. And as for the big boys, Dani Pedrosa
has braked so hard that you could plant a bush in the gap between the back
wheel of his Repsol Honda and the tarmac.

THE WATERFALL, SACHSENRING

The Sachsenring in Germany may be a legendary venue in the history books for the old road circuit and its vast crowds, but its modern-day counterpart boasts a truly special section. Turn 11, a fifth-gear right-hander, is followed by a stomach-churning plunge down the Waterfall before riders line up for the circuit's favourite overtaking spot at Turn 12.

Riders arrive at the fast right-hander before the Waterfall after being on the left side of the tyre for the previous seven bends. Cool morning practice sessions have caught out many a good man, while in the wet you have to be very brave. Here we see Repsol Honda team-mates Dani Pedrosa and Casey Stoner going over the edge in 2012.

THE CORKSCREW, LAGUNA SECA

Some decades ago, we Europeans became fed up with American riders telling us how the Corkscrew at Laguna Seca in California was the greatest modern-day bend in motorcycle racing. We expected so much when we finally arrived at the circuit for the US Grand Prix there, in 1988, and to say that we were not disappointed would be an understatement. Those Americans were not wrong.

This incredible sequence has a blind approach at the top of a hill before dropping off the face of the earth, plunging downhill through a right-hander followed by a left/right at the bottom. It is a truly iconic bend that staged one of the greatest overtaking moves of all time when Valentino Rossi went down the inside in the dirt to overtake Casey Stoner in 2008, as illustrated in the previous chapter. This scenic photo was taken three years earlier, showing Nicky Hayden, America's most recent World Champion, scoring his maiden MotoGP victory.

PART 4

THE RACING NATIONS

EIGHT NATIONAL STORIES

A multi-national audience enthralled by a multi-national sport – pre-race build-up at Catalunya in 2016.

CHAPTER 12
BRITAIN
THE BIT IN THE MIDDLE
BY NICK HARRIS

Like all good sagas, this particular story has an explosive start and a happy ending — the bit in the middle is the problem.

No wonder Britain was the birthplace of Grand Prix motorcycle racing. With post-war depression lifting slowly, any British sporting success was greeted with enormous patriotism and pride. Those emotions came in double doses as far as Grand Prix racing was concerned.

On 13 June 1949, on a giant granite rock in the middle of the Irish Sea, Grand Prix motorcycle racing was born. The roots were long-established. The TT races in the Isle of Man started way back in 1907 with the Manx government happy to close public roads to

RIGHT The very first World Championship event was held at the Isle of Man TT races in 1949.

allow riders to race their motorcycles. The first World Championship race was for 350cc machines and won by Freddie Frith riding the British-built Velocette. Four days later the very first 500cc World Championship race was staged and what a marathon it was. Consisting of seven tortuous laps round the legendary mountain circuit, the race, at 425 kilometres in length, was surely the most demanding and dangerous the sport has ever known.

How those British holidaymakers celebrated when Harold Daniell rode his Norton to success in just over three hours at an average speed of just under 140km/h. With British-built machinery filling all 35 finishing places, the stage was set for domination of the premier 500cc and 350cc classes of the new World Championship. Les Graham broke down on the Porcupine AJS while leading by over two minutes within sight of the chequered flag but made up by becoming the first 500cc World Champion with Frith taking the 350cc title.

A new name and hero arrived just a year later. With his slicked-back hair, Geoff Duke, the first rider to wear a one-piece leather suit, was a sporting legend riding for Norton. He won the Senior TT but finished second in the 500cc World Championship to Italian Umberto Masetti riding the magnificent four-cylinder Gilera. He also finished second in the 350cc title chase to Bob Foster on the Velocette but his time was coming.

In 1951 Duke won both the 350 and 500cc world titles, fighting off the mighty Gileras on his single-cylinder Nortons — but the tide was turning. The Italians started to turn the final screw on the British manufacturers and the decline of the British motorcycle industry, which had ruled the world, followed in turn. Duke stayed with Norton to retain the 350cc title a year later but lost the 500cc crown to Masetti. His move to the Gilera factory was inevitable if he was going to retain that World Champion status.

ABOVE Geoff Duke started his love affair with the Isle of Man by winning the Clubmans TT in 1949.

LEFT Harold Daniell won the first premier-class World Championship race at the Isle of Man in 1949.

In 1953 Duke brought Gilera the title in the 500cc class and a new Italian name was emerging with MV Agusta, better known for helicopter manufacturing. But MV's season was clouded in tragedy: that very first 500cc World Champion, Les Graham, was killed on the second lap of the TT riding one of the Italian machines.

Duke and Gilera then took over the 500cc crown for the next two years while Britain's manufacturing domination ended with a string of Moto Guzzi 350cc titles for British riders Fergus Anderson in 1953–54 and Bill Lomas in 1955–56. Goodbye Britain, welcome Italy — and soon Japan.

Although Britain was out of the manufacturers' battles for good, foreign factories often turned to British riders, who were still the best. John Surtees arrived from riding a Vincent around Brands Hatch to bring MV Agusta its first 500cc crown in 1956. He won both 350cc and 500cc world titles for Count Agusta for three successive years, 1958–60, before departing to four wheels, where he brought Ferrari the Formula One crown in 1964 – a World Championship double that has never been repeated.

It was like a conveyer belt of unbelievable talent as British riders simply ruled the roost. Perhaps the greatest of them all, Mike Hailwood, emerged from a privileged background to take over Surtees's mantle, winning four successive 500cc titles for MV. But by now the Japanese were also arriving and, like all other factories, they turned to British riders to bring them success.

Hailwood switched to Honda and promptly delivered

ABOVE John Surtees was the only man to win World Championships on two and four wheels; on motorcycles he won seven titles.

RIGHT Bill Ivy lightened up the sixties on and off the track.

ABOVE Sound of the sixties: Phil Read's two-stroke Yamaha leads Mike Hailwood's four-stroke Honda.

LEFT Mike Hailwood fires up the 500cc Honda at the start of one of the greatest TT races ever – the 1967 Senior on the Isle of Man.

ABOVE Barry Sheene brought Britain two world titles and put motorcycle racing on the front pages of the newspapers.

RIGHT Stephanie and Barry – the Beckhams of the seventies.

250cc and 350cc titles on those eardrum-piercing four-strokes. Yamaha turned up with its multi-cylinder two-strokes and with these Phil Read and Bill Ivy dominated the 125cc and 250cc classes. Read, surely one of the most underrated World Champions in the history of the sport, with seven titles to his name, later returned to win two 500cc world titles for MV Agusta. Dave Simmonds and Rod Gould continued the success story by winning 125cc and 250cc world titles respectively.

It seemed all you had to do was turn the page and a new World Champion would simply jump out, although the arrival of a certain Barry Sheene caught everybody by surprise. By 1976, when two-strokes were dominating the former four-stroke fortress of the 500cc class, the outspoken, long-haired, cigarette-smoking Londoner took Britain by storm, winning the 500cc World Championship in 1976 and 1977. Together with his great mate, Formula One World Champion James Hunt, Sheene put motorsport and motorcycling in particular on the front pages of every newspaper in the land. Their antics on and off the track, plus Sheene's bravery in recovering from life-threatening crashes, made them national heroes.

Massive crowds flocked to Silverstone to see Sheene in action for the very first British Grand Prix on the mainland, in 1977, the TT mountain circuit having been deemed too dangerous for Grand Prix racing. We sat back and waited for the success story to continue but unbelievably that was that. The book was slammed shut in our faces when a certain Kenny Roberts landed

from America in 1978 to lead a new revolution that did not include any pioneering British riders. For a nation that had spearheaded the first 29 years of Grand Prix racing by providing more World Champions and Grand Prix winners than any other nation, it was a remarkable situation that took 38 agonising years to rectify. So what happened to the new generation of budding Dukes, Hailwoods and Sheenes?

Roberts, having honed his skills on the dirt tracks of America, brought a new style to road racing and the Brits simply could not cope. While first the Americans and then the Australians thrived on the scary, sliding 500cc two-strokes, British riders brought up on a staple diet of road courses and short circuits simply could not match their pace. The likes of Ron Haslam and Niall Mackenzie came close to Grand Prix wins but never near a title, while others looked elsewhere for lucrative and successful employment. The World Superbike Championship was gaining momentum and British riders hoped for glory there.

Carl Fogarty received Sheene-like adulation when he won the title in the late nineties and was followed by the likes of Neil Hodgson and James Toseland. In the eyes of success-starved British fans, the World Superbike Championship had taken over from Grands Prix. In 2000 only 18,000 spectators attended the British Grand Prix at Donington Park while the British World Superbike round the same year attracted a crowd almost four times that size. Attempts to attract Fogarty to GPs failed and the trend continued.

FAR LEFT The first British Grand Prix on the British mainland was held at Silverstone in 1977.

LEFT Barry Sheene's last Grand Prix win came in the 1981 Swedish Grand Prix. Britain had to wait 35 long years before the next premier-class success.

Through Dorna's academy and then their championships, they took a clutch of young British talent to Spain under the masterful eye of Grand Prix winner Alberto Puig. From that strict regime the tide slowly started to turn. The likes of Bradley Smith and Scott Redding won 125cc GPs, later moving up through Moto2 to MotoGP. However, it was a Wiltshire lad who had learned his trade in the Dorna-backed Red Bull Rookies Cup that finally switched the lights back on in 2015. Danny Kent won the Moto3 World Championship to become the first British World Champion since Barry Sheene in 1977. The wait was finally over.

Kent's historic achievement was just the first few metres along a long road to recovery but another giant step was taken less than a year later, ironically from a rider who had progressed through the British and World Superbike Championships. Cal Crutchlow arrived from World Superbikes in 2011 and took time to adjust to the top MotoGP class. The last British rider to win in premier class was in 1981 when Sheene brought Yamaha victory at Anderstorp in Sweden. Like all good London buses, Crutchlow, riding the LCR Honda, came along twice in the space of two months to win in the Czech Republic and Australia. He also qualified on pole at his home Grand Prix at Silverstone, which attracted a weekend crowd of over 150,000. To add some icing to the cake, Scotsman John McPhee won the Moto3 Czech Republic race to make it a British double.

The recovery is underway but there is still a long way to go.

ABOVE Jeremy McWilliams brought Britain a rare victory in the 250cc race at the Dutch TT in 2001.

Britain remained in the darkness for those decades with just a few pinpricks of light piercing the all-encompassing gloom. Alan Carter, Ian McConnachie and Jeremy McWilliams kept the flickering Grand Prix flame burning against the Superbike furnace, but only just. While Spanish and Italian riders took over the mantle of the Americans and Australians in Grands Prix, it was Dorna who set the wheels in motion to bring back some success to the nation where it all started.

RIGHT At the 2008 British Grand Prix Scott Redding (centre) celebrates a 125cc victory that made him the youngest-ever Grand Prix winner. With him are Mike di Meglio (left), that year's 125cc champion, and Marc Márquez celebrating his first Grand Prix podium.

ABOVE Danny Kent became the first British World Champion for 38 years when he clinched the Moto3 title at the final round in Valencia in 2015.

LEFT At last… when Cal Crutchlow won the 2016 Czech Republic Grand Prix in Brno he became the first British premier-class Grand Prix winner for 35 years.

CHAPTER 13
SPAIN
PIONEERING TO THE TOP
BY EMILIO PÉREZ DE ROZAS

How did it all begin with racing in Spain? The same way it began in the rest of the world: through the efforts of true heroes, anonymous, leather-clad gladiators. These were men of courage and daring, impervious to fear. Take note of their names: Salvador Cañellas, Santiago Herrero, Ángel Nieto, Víctor Palomo, Benjamín Grau, Ricardo Tormo and others.

Montjuïc, 5 May 1968. Cañellas recalls his memories of that day: "It was the beginning of the Japanese bikes. Yamaha had a two-cylinder, way faster than our Bultaco. We were competing against engines with rotary valves that could go at least 50km/h faster than our bikes. I remember the race. I was running

RIGHT The first Spanish Grand Prix was held at Barcelona's legendary Montjuïc in 1951.

third when I suddenly saw that Phil Read's Yamaha had stopped, and a bit further down the track I found Bill Ivy's bike also stopped. I said to myself: 'This is your chance, Salvador!' And in the end, I won the race, with Ginger Molloy following me in second place."

This maiden triumph of a Spanish rider in the World Championship came three years after the first Grand Prix win for a Spanish machine, in Ulster for Bultaco with Molloy. Bultaco went on to win 28 Grands Prix in all and, just a month after Montjuïc, Derbi joined them as Grand Prix winners when Australian Barry Smith took victory in the 50cc race at the TT races on the Isle of Man. The Barcelona-based Derbi factory soon became a legend in the smaller classes with 106 more victories. Spanish riders continued risking their lives with their heroic efforts, because, as with all first-time experiences, danger lurked at every turn.

Cañellas remembers: "One weekend we were racing in Burriana, a small village in Castellón. I thought to myself, 'Salvador; you can't race here. You have to go to Europe.' Where I would have expected a racing course on an avenue, with wide turns and hay bales protecting the sides, there were these narrow streets, hardly a metre and a half wide. The final straight had tiles so polished that you could see your reflection in them. And, at the end of the course, there was a church and a wall two metres wide. I was astounded and scared by the danger we were facing there. It was not surprising at all that every year someone died there."

This world of leather and steel, the smell of gasoline and burned rubber, evolved with the times. The motorcycle racing madness grew, as did the fame of a roguish, smart, virtuous and extremely fast rider named Ángel Nieto. Spain was fertile ground for transforming this obscure sport into a phenomenon,

LEFT A historic 125cc moment occurred at Montjuïc in 1968 when Salvador Cañellas became Spain's first rider to win a Grand Prix on a Spanish motorcycle – Bultaco.

LEFT The Valencia circuit was named after 1978 50cc World Champion Ricardo Tormo.

RIGHT Jorge Martínez, nicknamed 'Aspar', achieved his first Grand Prix win in the 1984 80cc Dutch TT, riding for Derbi.

BELOW Ángel Nieto spearheaded the Spanish challenge in Grand Prix racing with his amazing 13 world titles.

as motorcycles had become increasingly popular and were used by thousands of people every day, especially in Catalonia. Motorcycle manufacturers such as Derbi and outstanding riders like Grau, Tormo, Sito Pons, Jorge Martínez ('Áspar'), Manuel 'Champi' Herreros, Joan Garriga and Álex Crivillé contributed to its growth.

Among so many winners and champions, it is impossible to pick out a single individual who started it all. The story told by Cañellas — a rider who later moved into car racing and became a superb driver — shows the merit of being the first. But it is clear that the foundation for the boom of two-wheeled motorsport was laid by the *agent provocateur* of this movement, the legendary '12+1' Ángel Nieto.

Nieto made television believe in the sport and, with television as an ally, everything else fell in line. Television can achieve anything for a sports discipline, and we now marvel at the great progress it has brought with it for fans, such as onboard cameras and 360-degree swivel lenses.

The incredible duels between Sito Pons and Joan Garriga in 250cc — Honda *versus* Yamaha — made

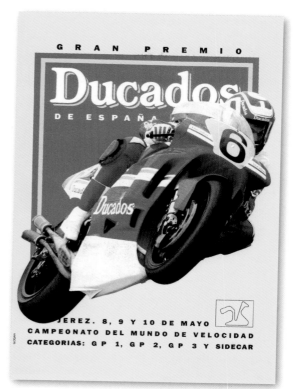

LEFT This is the programme cover for the Spanish Grand Prix held at Jerez in 1992, the first year of the Dorna era.

BELOW Sito Pons was the first Spanish 250cc World Champion, taking the title in 1988 and again in 1989, then became a successful team owner.

ABOVE Álex Crivillé rewrote the Spanish history books when he because the country's first premier-class World Champion in 1999.

RIGHT Dani Pedrosa celebrates his 125cc title at Sepang in 2003.

audiences at the races and watching at home on television leap from their seats. In 1999 Crivillé opened the doors at the top level, 'the Everest' of motorcycle racing, when he became the first Spanish 500cc champion. From that moment on, everything became a little easier for the rest. The great merit of these pioneers is that they achieved everything on their own, when nobody believed they could, or even really knew this sport well.

The courage of a man like Alberto Puig is evident, leading the school of champions that gave us Dani Pedrosa, and starting the national Spanish promotional championship, an event praised and imitated worldwide. Nobody would deny its significance. It has now become part of a motorcycle racing powerhouse, supported by sponsors, great race tracks, organization and money.

Remember also the resolve and determination of Sete Gibernau, who pushed Valentino Rossi so hard but had to settle for second place in the points standings in 2003 and 2004, and Toni Elías, MotoGP winner and the very first Moto2 World Champion. Both were pioneers in their own right.

LEFT Jorge Lorenzo
won the first of his five
world titles in 2006 when
he clinched the 250cc
crown in Valencia.

ABOVE Marc Márquez won the 2012 Moto2 title before moving to the MotoGP class with stunning success.

RIGHT Spanish fans celebrate more home success at Jerez.

The rivalry and competition between Jorge Lorenzo and Marc Márquez has captivated fans all over the world, in what many consider a return of the legendary battles of Pons and Garriga. The uncanny ability of Márquez to revolutionize the MotoGP category is an unprecedented feat, with his fine attitude and other-worldly racing skills. He was able to face and defeat a titan like Valentino Rossi, becoming the youngest-ever champion, double champion and triple champion.

But if we are to pay homage to the forefathers of this 'wonderful madness', the ones who put Spanish motorcycle racing on the top of the world, I would vote for the pioneers, the original madmen. Racing over cobblestones, with less powerful bikes, dashing between trees and sometimes crashing at the church doors on the finish line.

As Salvador Cañellas remembers: "Those humble beginnings are as similar to the modern racing spectacle as an Olivetti typewriter is to a modern computer."

To me, those early pioneers set the true benchmarks to which our modern champions can aspire.

ABOVE The magnificent grandstand at the Circuit de Barcelona-Catalunya – one of four Spanish circuits on the MotoGP calendar in the modern era.

LEFT The final race of Dorna's first 25 years was fittingly in Spain, at Valencia.

CHAPTER 14
JAPAN
RECOVERY TO DOMINATION
BY SATOSHI ENDO

The history of Japanese motorcycle racing began in 1955 with the Mount Asama volcano race in Karuizawa, Nagano, a village located at the foot of this active volcano. The riders started at 30-second intervals, as at the Isle of Man TT, and the 19.2-kilometre course on compressed volcanic ash was just like an enduro race track with some jumps. Over 10,000 fans from all over the country came to see the action.

The main events, senior 500cc and junior 350cc, were dominated by Honda. The lightweight class (250cc) was the hardest-fought among various manufacturers such as Honda, Lilac and Pointer (the latter two companies no longer exist). In the ultra-lightweight category (125cc) Yamaha had a monopoly

BELOW Where it all started – the Mount Fuji race.

of the podium positions after a cut-throat battle with Honda and Suzuki.

At that time there were over 100 motorcycle manufacturers in Japan. The industry's post-war economic expansion, however, vanished with the arrival of deflation, and consequently the number of motorcycle companies halved and those that did not disappear struggled for survival. This was one of the factors that led some manufacturers to start developing motorsport models in parallel to the production of motorcycles for daily use.

In 1954, a year before the inaugural Mount Asama volcano race, Honda announced its intention to participate in the Isle of Man TT. Soichiro Honda, founder of Honda Motor Co., Ltd., declared the following: "My dream is to win the races all over the world with the vehicles I develop. To make this dream come true, it is indispensable that our activities become stable and, moreover, we need to introduce high-precision machineries and superb designs. We observe an outstanding technological advance in the world. But, now I am strongly convinced that we can win if we fully use our own inspiration. Finally, we have production facilities and we are confident of their capacity. And now, we have decided to participate in the Isle of Man TT. Although no Japanese rider has taken part in this race before, if we win or finish the race with our machine, we can show Honda's motorcycle excellence to the world. The motorcycle manufacturing business is a culmination in modern heavy industry and it requires comprehensive technologies. We are urged to have the highest level technical solutions not only for the production of the power unit, but also the development of tyres, drive chains, and carburettors. The true value of Japanese industry will be tested here and we must show the high level of our technology to the world. Honda's mission is to enhance the industries of Japan."

During the next few years, Honda used its

ABOVE Soichiro Honda (centre with glasses) celebrates with his racing friends before setting out to conquer the world.

LEFT Kunimitsu Takahashi won the 1961 250cc German Grand Prix at Hockenheim to become the first Grand Prix winner from Japan.

SUZUKA CIRCUIT/NOV. 1. 1964
2nd JAPAN GRAND-PRIX RACE MEETING
MOTORCYCLE FEDERATION OF JAPAN
1964年11月1日/鈴鹿サーキット
OFFICIAL PROGRAMME
第2回日本グランプリレース・プログラム

●LUIGI TAVERI ●MIKE DUFF ●ERNST DEGNER
●TARQUINIO PROVINI ●PHIL READ ●ALAN SHEPHERD
●MIKE HAILWOOD ●RALPH BRYANS ●HUGH ANDERSON
●JIM REDMAN ●FUMIO ITO

昭和の
ショック・アブソーバー

ABOVE Fumio Ito leads Phil Read and Jim Redman in the 1963 250cc Japanese Grand Prix at Suzuka. Ito eventually finished second behind Redman.

RIGHT What a line-up for the 1964 Japanese Grand Prix at Suzuka.

experience in the Mount Asama volcano race to guide development of its competition models, and finally, in 1959, five years after the 'Announcement of Participation in The Isle of Man TT', the company appeared in the 125cc class for the first time, with four Japanese riders. Honda's quartet finished the full race distance after a battle with European machines — MV, MZ and Ducati — and their performance was rewarded with the team prize. Honda duly became a regular participant in World Championship motorcycle racing, and Suzuki and Yamaha quickly followed.

The first Grand Prix victory by a Japanese rider came in 1961, when Honda's Kunimitsu Takahashi won the 250cc West German Grand Prix at Hockenheim, and that year he also won the 125cc Ulster Grand Prix. A year later Takahashi looked to be a prospective World Champion when he scored two successive 125cc victories at the opening rounds in Spain and France, but then he suffered serious injuries in the third round, the Isle of Man TT, and the honour of a first Japanese World Champion title had to wait. Takahashi continued his racing activities on four wheels, becoming one of Japan's best drivers and competing in the Japanese

round of the Formula One World Championship in 1977. Nowadays he is a legendary figure on the Japanese motorsport scene and manages a car racing team in national events.

In 1961 Honda celebrated its first World Championship titles, achieved by Tom Phillis and Mike Hailwood, in the 125cc and 250cc classes respectively, in addition to the constructors' titles in both categories. This is when Honda's glorious racing career took off.

In 1963 Suzuki factory rider Mitsuo Itoh became the first Japanese winner at the Isle of Man TT when he won the ultra-lightweight class. Itoh took his second Grand Prix victory at Fuji in Japan in 1967. After his retirement from motorcycle racing, he also transferred to car racing and during the nineties he managed the Suzuki factory 500cc racing team.

In the early sixties the Suzuka circuit, the first full-scale race track in Japan, was constructed by Honda. It hosted the Japanese Grand Prix in 1963 and the succeeding two years. After that, another new circuit, Fuji International Speedway, was completed and this hosted the Grand Prix in 1966 and 1967.

The Japanese motorcycle racing industry became

ABOVE Jim Redman winning the 1964 Lightweight TT for Honda. The Rhodesian spearheaded Honda's World Championship success with 45 Grand Prix wins for the Japanese factory.

BELOW Japan's first World Champion was Takazumi Katayama, who won the 350cc title in 1977.

ABOVE Tadahiko Taira lines up his Yamaha (21) on the front row of the grid for the 1987 Swedish Grand Prix at Anderstorp.

a pioneer of the Japanese industrial might that was expanding throughout the world. In 1966, just six years after that first challenge in the Isle of Man TT, Honda accomplished the extraordinary achievement of sweeping the constructors' titles in all categories (50cc, 125cc, 250cc, 350cc and 500cc).

RIGHT What a day for the Aoki brothers at Suzuka in 1995: Takuma was third in the 500 race, Nobuatsu second in the 250 and Haruchika won the 125.

Many Japanese riders emerged during this period and produced good results. Yamaha's Fumio Ito, known as 'genius' within the factory team, secured Yamaha's first Grand Prix victory in the 250cc class at the 1963 Belgian Grand Prix. Yamaha's other Japanese rider, Hiroshi Hasegawa, also showed his talent alongside Ito with one 250cc victory. At Suzuki, Yoshimi Katayama enjoyed one 125cc victory and three in the 50cc class in 1966 and 1967, finishing second in the 50cc World Championship in 1967 before switching to four wheels, while Isao Morishita had one 50cc victory. At Honda, Teisuke Tanaka achieved one 125cc victory and played a key role among Honda riders throughout these years.

Alongside its motorcycle racing, Honda also competed in the Formula One World Championship from 1963 to 1969. However, with the arrival of new regulations to control exhaust emissions, followed by the oil crisis of 1973, the company was forced to concentrate its resources on car production and suspended all racing activity, in both motorcycling and Formula One. During the seventies, while Honda was absent, Yamaha and Suzuki continued, and Kawasaki made its début.

In this period, two-stroke engine technology was in its heyday. Yamaha demonstrated its remarkable potential and, in 1974, conquered the constructors' title in four categories: 125cc, 250cc, 350cc and 500cc. In 1975 Giacomo Agostini brought Yamaha its first 500cc World Championship title. That same year, Hideo Kanaya, whose first win had been in the 250cc West German Grand Prix of 1972, joined Yamaha as Agostini's team-mate in the 350cc and 500cc classes, and became the first Japanese rider to score a premier-class Grand Prix victory, at Austria's Salzburgring in 1975.

There were many other outstanding riders who raced for Japanese factory teams but never stood on the top step of the podium: Ikujiro Takai (Yamaha), Hiroyuki Kawasaki (Suzuki) and Akihito Kiyohara (Kawasaki) played their part in Japanese success in this period and remain unforgettable heroic figures for their fans at home.

At last, in 1977, Japan acquired its first World Champion when Takazumi Katayama won the 350cc title with five race wins on his Yamaha.

Honda returned to World Championship motorcycle racing in the eighties. By this time, the four big Japanese motorcycle manufacturers — Honda, Yamaha, Suzuki and Kawasaki — were dominating the world market, and finally all four fought shoulder-to-shoulder in Grands Prix for the first time. Later, Kawasaki, which showed considerable strength in the 250cc and 350cc classes, withdrew, but the tough battle between Honda, Yamaha and Suzuki continued.

One man who gave a tremendous boost to Japanese

racing fever was Tadahiko Taira. The Yamaha rider won just one Grand Prix, at San Marino in 1986 in the 250cc class, but he displayed his great talent in the 500cc class as a Yamaha factory rider. Taira's force of personality attracted many star riders, including World Champions Wayne Rainey and Eddie Lawson, to the Suzuka Eight Hours endurance race, helping to turn it into a major event, and he also played a part in the resumption of the Japanese Grand Prix at the same circuit in 1987. Taira was undeniably a superstar in Japanese racing and his popularity helped to motivate a new generation of Japanese riders.

The number of Japanese Grand Prix riders and their level of achievement increased dramatically in this period. At the Japanese Grand Prix home-grown racers dominated the podium for several years, especially in the 125cc and 250cc classes.

In the 125cc class, Noboru Ueda (Honda), Kazuto Sakata (Honda and Aprilia), Takeshi Tsujimura (Honda), Masaki Tokudome (Honda), Haruchika Aoki (Honda), Masao Azuma (Honda) and Youichi Ui (Yamaha, Aprilia and Derbi) were all involved in battles for the title. Sakata won it in 1994 and 1998 and Aoki in 1995 and 1996.

BELOW The youngest of the Aoki racing brothers, Haruchika, brought the family – and Japan – two 125cc world titles.

ABOVE The majestic Daijiro Kato dominated the 2001 250cc World Championship.

RIGHT There were three Japanese winners at the 2000 Japanese Grand Prix – Norick Abe (500), Daijiro Kato (250) and Youichi Ui (125).

In the 250cc class, Tetsuya Harada (Yamaha and Aprilia) won the title in 1993, while Tadayuki Okada (Honda), Nobuatsu Aoki (Honda), Shinya Nakano (Yamaha) and Osamu Miyazaki (Yamaha) also achieved Grand Prix wins.

In the 500cc class, Tadayuki Okada (Honda) took four victories and Norifumi Abe (Yamaha), who made his début when he was only 18, achieved three. Two of the three Aoki brothers, Nobuatsu and Takuma, also participated in this class and celebrated by standing on the podium together.

At the dawn of the new millennium, Daijiro Kato (Honda) débuted in the 250cc class and became a World Champion in 2001, setting a new record by winning 11 GPs that year. The close battle for the title between Kato and Tetsuya Harada (Aprilia) showed the superb prowess of Japanese riders to the whole world.

A golden era for Japanese riders emerged in the premier class. Toru Ukawa (Honda) and Makoto Tamada (Honda) both stood on the top step of the podium. Also, the likes of Daijiro Kato (Honda), Norifumi Abe (Yamaha), Noriyuki Haga (Yamaha and Aprilia), Shinya Nakano (Yamaha), Tetsuya Harada (Aprilia) and

Nobuatsu Aoki (Suzuki and Proton) made their mark.

In 2003, Kato tragically lost his life after crashing in the Japanese Grand Prix. In honour of his remarkable career, Kato became a MotoGP legend and his number 74 was officially retired. In the 250cc class, Yuki Takahashi (Honda) took two wins and Hiroshi Aoyama won nine GPs and brought Honda the final 250cc World Championship in 2009. In the first year of the new Moto2 class, 2010, Shoya Tomizawa (Suter) and Yuki Takahashi (Tech3) took victories. Not until Takaaki Nakagami (Kalex) grabbed first place in Moto2 at the Dutch TT in 2016 was there another Japanese winner.

Until around 2000 Japanese manufacturers supported young national riders so that they could challenge in GPs, but at about this time the factory teams started to withdraw from national competitions and gradually a door closed. However, Honda established a scholarship for outstanding young talent from domestic teams to send them upwards to World Championship racing. This scholarship enabled Grand Prix winners Yuki Takahashi and Hiroshi Aoyama to display their talents on the world stage.

Today, Honda and Dorna collaborate in the search for and development of junior talent with the Idimitsu Asia Talent Cup and the Red Bull Rookies MotoGP Cup. We are already witnessing the birth of new champions not only from Japan but from other Asian countries. It goes without saying that MotoGP will always be the prime objective for all up-and-coming Japanese motorcycle racers.

ABOVE In 2009 Hiroshi Aoyama was the winner of the last 250cc World Championship.

BELOW Shoya Tomizawa won the very first Moto2 Grand Prix at Qatar in 2010.

CHAPTER 15
ITALY
PASSION AND STYLE
BY ENRICO BORGHI

O n the façade of Rome's Palazzo della Civiltà Italiana, construction of which began in 1937 and finished after the Second World War, the following sentence is inscribed in big block capitals: "A nation of poets, artists, heroes, saints, thinkers, scientists, navigators and migrants." When those unmovable and popular words were carved into stone, the motorcycle World Championship did not exist, but, a little later, in 1949 a story began that has gone on to become an epic. It could be added, therefore, that Italians are a nation of bikers as well…

Throughout the world, no countries can rival Italy for motorcycling passion, which is widespread and ever-lasting. Despite the fluctuations of time, including the Second World War, Italy has managed, decade after decade, to remain at or near the top in terms of both riders and manufacturing. Italy has contributed all the various elements related to motorcycles and racing: from motorcycles to components, from engineers to designers, from mechanics to managers, from protective clothing to financial backers, from teams to organizers — and, of course, circuits and riders. That's why in Italy we speak of "the culture of the bike" more than in any other country: motorcycling is rooted in society and has become part of people's lives. Everyone is familiar with motorcycle brands and the names of the top racers. People talk about motorcycles and riders in factories and offices, in streets and bars, in cities and in holiday resorts, men and women, young and old. Valentino Rossi once said: "My greatest satisfaction is that among my fans there are mothers and grandmothers who watch my races while making pasta in the kitchen!" As for popularity in Italy, Formula One and Grand Prix motorcycle racing come just after football.

To understand Italian achievement in motorcycle racing, you just need to look at some numbers, as at the end of 2016. In terms of road racing, the most important discipline, Italy has produced the highest number of solo World Champion riders, 75, compared with 46 from Spain and 45 from Britain. Italy is also the country that has won the highest number of solo races, 762, while Spaniards have won 551 and Britons 402.

In terms of manufacturing, only Italy comes close to Japan, with 91 constructors' titles compared with 126. Also, Italy is the nation with the highest number of motorcycle manufacturers to have won at least one world title, 11, a number far ahead of Germany (five) and Japan (four).

Engine, car and motorcycle culture has produced a proliferation of engineers, industrialists, race circuits

BELOW The Palazzo della Civiltà Italiana in Rome — the inscription on its façade could apply to the nation's motorcycle racing heroes.

LEFT Umberto Masetti brought Gilera its first 500cc world title in 1950 and won another two years later.

and — ultimately — riders and drivers. Although the start of the motorcycle boom goes back to the dawn of the 20th century, it was only after the Second World War that real lift-off took place. Beyond the enormous number of Italian riders and manufacturers, a few further points should be observed: the weather in Italy is ideal, as is its landscape; there is a history and culture of sport dating back to Ancient Rome and its concept of the stadium, exemplified by the Coliseum; and the Italian national character specializes in creative imagination, art and entrepreneurship.

Added to that is a passionate gift for story-telling and history. Race coverage has become increasingly epic thanks to the talented journalists and writers who have produced reporting loaded with heroic connotations. Television paved the way for heroes such as Giacomo Agostini to achieve ever-greater popularity.

In the first half of the 20th century there were three main Italian brands: Gilera, Bianchi and Guzzi, all based in Milan, Lombardy, where there also existed the only permanent race track in Italy. The *autodromo* at Monza, constructed in 1922, was created to demonstrate the products of an emerging domestic industry in cars and

LEFT The Monza circuit staged the first Nations Grand Prix in the first year of the World Championship.

motorcycles. In fact Monza increasingly became territory for four wheels rather than two.

In May 1973, due to the accident in which Jarno Saarinen and Renzo Pasolini died, it became clear that Monza was too dangerous for bikes because they had become so fast. This was fortunate for Imola, situated in Emilia Romagna, which was gaining more and more industrial importance. The area now known as 'Motor Valley' includes Emilia, with its hub of great car manufacturers (Ferrari, Maserati and Lamborghini), Romagna, specializing in motorcycle manufacturing (Ducati has strong influences from Romagna although it is actually located in Emilia), and the northern part of Marche, very close to the border with Romagna, where Benelli, Morbidelli and Motobi are situated — and Franco Uncini and Valentino Rossi were born in this region.

In these parts of the country, boys often grew up as apprentices in motorcycle repair shops, dreaming of becoming riders, and many of them made those dreams come true. Later, as parents, they encouraged their children to ride 'minibikes', which have proved a fertile training ground in this region more than anywhere else. It is from the 'minibike' world that, among others, Valentino Rossi, Marco Simoncelli, Andrea Dovizioso and Marco Melandri have emerged, as well as many of the youngsters now in Moto3 and Moto2.

Italian motorcycling developed firstly on the road, then on the track. Originally, any wide road became an opportunity for motorcycles — and cars — to race in a landscape where in fact every single road could turn

ABOVE Carlo Ubbiali dominated the smaller classes during the fifties, winning nine world titles.

RIGHT Libero Liberati won four Grands Prix in 1957 to secure the 500cc World Championship for Gilera.

into a track. Emilia Romagna boasted the mother of all roads, Via Emilia, built by the Romans in 189 BC. Via Emilia was designed to link Rimini (in the south of Romagna, very close to Marche) with Piacenza (in the north of Emilia, at the border with Lombardy) and this artery has allowed life, culture and business activities to flow throughout Italy, for centuries, even millennia. It can be considered the first highway in history and so you can imagine it also as the first race track.

If you share the theory that the first tracks were the roads themselves, it is interesting to note that at some point every town in Emilia Romagna had its own road course, and some even managed to build their own permanent tracks, as was the case in Modena, Imola, Misano and Parma (at Varano de' Melegari), not to mention nearby Mugello, just a few kilometres away in Tuscany, on the border.

The first races took place on street tracks in the inland territories of Faenza and Ravenna and then moved to the coast from Cesenatico and Cervia to Rimini and Riccione. The races were a spectacle for the fans, an excellent training ground for World Championship riders (many non-Italian stars rode here

ABOVE Classic Italy: Giacomo Agostini in action on the 500cc MV Agusta in three-cylinder form as raced from 1966 onwards.

LEFT The 1973 Grand Prix in Italy can only be remembered for the crash that killed Jarno Saarinen and Renzo Pasolini.

ABOVE Marco Lucchinelli brought Suzuki the 1981 500cc world title before switching to Honda.

RIGHT Franco Uncini continued the Suzuki success story when he became 500cc World Champion in 1982.

too), plus they were promotional and entrepreneurial events. As reports about the events ended up in newspapers they contributed to attracting more people to the Adriatic coast. This is why, in 2007, some of the towns on the Riviera, where 50 years earlier riders raced along the streets, founded a company and invested a significant amount of money to organize the Misano MotoGP race — history repeating itself.

Misano was the last track to be built in the area in 1972 because the great era of street racing was coming to an end. A year earlier, the tragic death in Riccione of Angelo Bergamonti, who fell while competing against Agostini, marked the end of races on the roads in Italy. This was in the Mototemporada Romagnola race, a popular event composed of a series of road races run in the spring between 1945 and 1971 in Milano Marittima, Lugo, Cesenatico, Rimini, Riccione, Cattolica and Modena.

Naturally the factories supported the most talented riders. In the long period of Italian post-war motorcycling strength, the main manufacturers were Gilera, Mondial, MV Agusta and Moto Guzzi, then, after a period of transition in the 1990s, Aprilia and Ducati arrived.

ABOVE Fausto Gresini won 21 Grands Prix and two 125cc world titles before becoming an equally successful team owner.

LEFT Imola hosted the 500th World Championship 500cc race in 1996.

ABOVE Marco Melandri dominated 250cc Grands Prix in 2002 with nine wins on his way to the world title.

RIGHT Andrea Dovizioso riding to second place in the 125cc Malaysian Grand Prix in 2004 and world title glory that year.

The 1990s also saw a slight decrease in the number of Italian Grand Prix victories, although riders such as Marco Lucchinelli, Luca Cadalora and Fausto Gresini still managed to win important races. But, if the riders were having less success, the factories and a new generation of managers and talent scouts (some of whom were former riders) kept developing, and television continued to ensure broad coverage. That is why the Italian racing fraternity was able, in that less successful period, to prepare the ground for a great return to the top.

At the time when Dorna began to organize the World Championship from 1992, Loris Capirossi started to achieve success, followed by Max Biaggi and, a little later, Valentino Rossi. After them came a series of Italian riders who became World Champions: Alessandro Gramigni, Marco Melandri, Andrea Dovizioso and Marco Simoncelli — plus Manuel Poggiali from San Marino. So everyone in Italy became heavily involved in motorcycling. Riders appeared on prime-time talk shows and bikes became the subject of economic and industrial conferences, as well as lectures at universities.

It is fair to call it the Italian Renaissance of the motorcycle.

ABOVE A sea of yellow in the Tuscan hills – Valentino Rossi fans making their presence felt in Mugello.

BELOW Marco Simoncelli clinches the 250cc World Championship at Sepang in 2008.

CHAPTER 16
USA
HAPPY DAYS
BY PAUL CARRUTHERS

Ask an American road race fan when Grand Prix motorcycle racing started to mean something to them and the response you will likely get is 1978. Or the year of King Kenny. Most Americans would tell you that GP racing began with the first of Kenny Roberts's three straight 500cc World Championships that year, but they would be wrong. The history of Grand Prix racing in the US dates back to 1964 and 1965 with Mike Hailwood winning back-to-back US GPs on an MV Agusta at Daytona International Speedway.

Thus there are really two parts when discussing the history of Grand Prix motorcycle racing in the US: American riders and American rounds. Although the 23-year gap between the US hosting a round of the World Championship at Daytona to the race returning to American soil at Laguna Seca in 1988 was a long one, the success of American riders in the series was at a high during that drought of US GPs.

Simply put, Americans dominated the 500cc World Championship from 1978 to 1993, winning 13 titles with Kenny Roberts, Freddie Spencer, Eddie Lawson, Wayne Rainey and Kevin Schwantz earning those crowns. Then the well started to dry up, with Kenny Roberts Jr's lone title in 2000 coming seven years after Schwantz's. Then came another six-year drought between Roberts Jr's title and Nicky Hayden's in 2006.

RIGHT He came, he saw, he conquered – Kenny Roberts opened the Grand Prix floodgates for American riders.

LEFT Randy Mamola in action on the 500cc Suzuki near the Russian border at the Imatra circuit in Finland.

LEFT Freddie Spencer finished second here at Spa in 1983 but went on to win his first 500cc world title that year.

ABOVE Eddie Lawson won the United States Grand Prix at Laguna Seca in 1988.

RIGHT The Laguna Seca race in 1988 marked the return of the World Championship to America after a 23-year break.

And that's it. Americans have not won a title since Hayden's. Ten years. An eternity.

As for US Grands Prix, there have been 27 of those since the two at Daytona in 1964 and 1965: 15 at Laguna Seca, eight at Indianapolis Motor Speedway and four at Circuit Of The Americas. None has been bigger than the first: the 1988 US Grand Prix at Laguna.

While American riders dominated the sport, American race fans had no real way of watching them — especially not live. That changed in 1988 when Grand Prix motorcycle racing made its way back to American shores and to California's Monterey Peninsula. It quickly became the biggest road race in the US and the script from that first race was straight out of Hollywood.

Schwantz opened that season with the first 500cc GP victory of his career, at Suzuka, bringing even more interest to US fans in GP racing as the Schwantz/Rainey rivalry had been transferred to the GPs, the duo joining Lawson, Randy Mamola and Mike Baldwin in the premier class. Two weeks after the Japanese opener, the series rolled into Laguna Seca for the first time, with Lawson scoring victory. Rainey was fourth, after taking

pole position, Schwantz fifth and Baldwin 10th. Four Americans in the top ten. And not really a surprise.

The shocker, however, was in the 250cc class. This is what made that first US GP so special. An American won that too, but it was not John Kocinski. Instead, a little fella with a big heart by the name of Jimmy Filice showed up for a one-off race on a factory Honda NSR250 and went out and dominated, beating the likes of Sito Pons, Dominique Sarron and Kocinski, who qualified on pole position. The diminutive Californian won the race by nearly 10 seconds with Kocinski a disappointed fourth and fifth-placed Bubba Shobert the third American in the top ten. In those two races at Laguna Seca, American race fans saw American riders totally dominate. Not a bad début.

And it was little different in the 1989 US Grand Prix. This time Kocinski won the 250cc GP with Filice second. And Rainey won his first race of the season at his home track. Eddie Lawson was crowned the 1989 500cc World Champion. American race fans were getting used to this. Life was good.

Kocinski won his home GP again in 1990. Ditto for Rainey. Both would go on to become World Champions

ABOVE **ABOVE** Jim Filice took his only Grand Prix victory in the 250cc race at Laguna Seca in 1988.

LEFT Eddie Lawson after winning the German Grand Prix in 1986, the year he won the second of his four 500cc World Championships.

RIGHT John Kocinski won the 1990 250cc World Championship before switching to the 500cc class a year later with Kenny Roberts's Yamaha team.

BELOW Bitter rivals at home and in the 500cc World Championship – Wayne Rainey (World Champion in 1990–92) and Kevin Schwantz (World Champion in 1993).

that year and American GP racers truly ruled the world.

In 1991, the Grand Prix came to Laguna Seca with Kocinski now in the 500cc class as Rainey's team-mate. And he came in talking big. He left in handcuffs, having irked a police officer by speeding out of Laguna Seca after crashing out of his brief battle with Rainey in the GP. Rainey won and again he would march to the title, his second in a row.

In 1992, there was not a US Grand Prix at Laguna Seca. Or anywhere for that matter.

The race returned in 1993 but it did so under a dark cloud with Rainey suffering his career-ending injury the week prior in Italy. Racing went on, but it lacked the lustre of previous years even though Kocinski took victory on home soil on the factory Cagiva. Schwantz would win his lone World Championship that year, but it would be the last for seven years for America as that era of dominance came to a close.

In 1994, it got even worse. The tide turned completely at the US GP, as an American failed to win for the first time in the six-year history of the race. Victory instead went to Italian Luca Cadalora. For American fans who had been spoiled by American success, it was a dose of reality. Coincidentally, it also marked the temporary end of the Laguna Seca event and it would be 11 years before it returned.

When it did return, it did so in the best way possible — with an American winner. Nicky Hayden raced to victory in 2005 on his four-stroke MotoGP Honda as the hills of the Monterey Peninsula again reverberated with

ABOVE Wayne Rainey returned to the paddock as a team manager in 1994.

LEFT World Superbike Champion Colin Edwards was one of the most popular American riders to compete in Grand Prix racing.

Red Bull Indianapolis GP

OFFICIAL PROGRAM

motogp.com

SEPTEMBER 14, 2008 $10

RIGHT Nearly 100 years after its construction, the fabled Indianapolis Motor Speedway staged its first significant motorcycle race, in 2008.

The US Grand Prix ran at Laguna Seca for seven more years after Hayden's two wins, but none of those featured an American winner. The win list instead reads: Casey Stoner, Valentino Rossi, Dani Pedrosa, Jorge Lorenzo, Stoner again and again, and finally in 2013 a young Marc Márquez won his first race at Laguna in what would mark the end of the championship visits to Monterey. The racing there has continued with MotoAmerica and World Superbike racing, but MotoGP has left and it is unlikely to be coming back.

But there is plenty of life left in the race. In fact, America staged two GPs in the period 2008–2012, three in 2013, and two again in 2014–2015 — something that seemed impossible even in the years of American dominance in MotoGP. Initially, the two races were held at Laguna and the most famous race place in the world, Indianapolis Motor Speedway, home of the Indy 500. Then came the Circuit Of The Americas (COTA) and Indy. Now it is just COTA.

The first-ever MotoGP at Indy was won fittingly by Rossi, the most popular Grand Prix racer in the US — at least since Roberts Jr. Lorenzo followed suit with a win at Indy, then came victories by Pedrosa, Stoner, Pedrosa again and three in a row by Márquez, the Spaniard shutting the door on both Laguna and Indy with victories.

In 2013, Márquez opened the doors to Circuit Of The Americas with victory and he has kept that streak alive at the Texas-sized facility in Austin.

the sound of race bikes. The win was a boost to Grand Prix racing in the US and it would continue a year later when Hayden won not only won the US GP but also the World Championship. Life for American GP fans was good again.

But it did not last.

RIGHT Nicky Hayden, the 2006 MotoGP World Champion, celebrates his 200th Grand Prix appearance with proud Mum and Dad.

The COTA round is still popular with American race fans who keep pace with the series on a weekly basis through live television coverage, even though currently there are no Americans racing in the series. The on-track action is top-notch, the rivalries intense. And American race fans still have Rossi to cheer for — with some even switching alliances to Márquez and Lorenzo in preparation for a future without Rossi.

But reality sets in quickly when you realize that an American has not won a MotoGP race since 25 June 2011, when Texan Ben Spies claimed victory at Assen in the Netherlands. Since then it has been the Neverlands.

Although it is a far cry from the early days of Lawson, Rainey, Schwantz, Kocinski and the rest racing and winning in the hills of Monterey, MotoGP remains hugely popular in the US and the only thing missing is American racers. But MotoAmerica, the new home of the AMA Superbike Series, is hopeful of producing young American racers who will one day move to the world stage and MotoGP. Ironically, that series is spearheaded by a blast from the past — three-time 500cc World Champion Wayne Rainey.

Let's see where the future takes us.

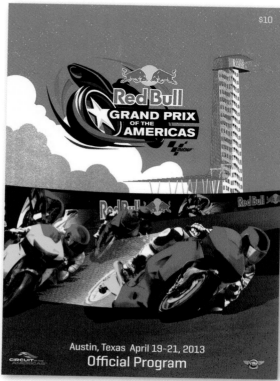

ABOVE & LEFT The fantastic venue of COTA – Circuit Of The Americas – brought Grand Prix racing to Texas in 2013.

CHAPTER 17
AUSTRALIA
AGAINST THE ODDS
BY DON COX

When Jack Miller surged to victory in a rain-lashed 2016 Dutch TT, he added another chapter to Australia's remarkable Grand Prix story.

A nation today of just under 25 million and one that has never had a volume-production motorcycle industry or provided high levels of home sponsorship for its riders has, nonetheless, claimed almost a quarter of the premier-class victories in the Dorna era.

Only Spain and Italy have more wins than Australia's 98 by Michael Doohan, Wayne Gardner, Daryl Beattie, Garry McCoy, Troy Bayliss, Casey Stoner, Chris Vermeulen and Miller in the 406 Grands Prix from 1992 to 2016 inclusive. Valentino Rossi has topped the individual premier-class winners' table of the past 25 years on 88. The next three on the list are Doohan, Jorge Lorenzo and Stoner.

In overall Grand Prix history, Australia held fourth place on the all-time premier-class victory table until the middle of the 2016 season, when its total of 125 was eclipsed by Spain. It is also fifth on the table of all-time solo victories.

Miller was the 12th Australian to win a premier-class classic and the first MotoGP rider in a decade to win on a satellite machine. Only traditional Grand Prix powerhouses Italy and Britain have had more individual victors in the main class.

RIGHT Early pioneer Arthur Simcock (right) won the 350cc race at the 1930 Dutch TT 19 years before the World Championship even started.

ABOVE Keith Campbell was the first Australian World Champion, winning the 1957 350cc title on the Moto Guzzi.

LEFT Kel Carruthers may have masterminded Kenny Roberts's three world titles but a decade earlier, in 1969, he won the 250cc world title.

RIGHT When Wayne
Gardner won the 1987
500cc World Championship
he sent Australia wild.

Across all solo classes, 19 Australians have collectively won 180 Grands Prix and six have been World Champions, including five titles in succession for Doohan (1994–1998) and Stoner bookending the 800 era (2007–2011) in both race and championship victories.

The other champions were Keith Campbell (Moto Guzzi 350 in 1957), Tom Phillis (Honda 125 in 1961), Kel Carruthers (Benelli 250 in 1969) and Gardner (Honda 500 in 1987). Those four sealed their titles at long-supplanted venues — Dundrod in Northern Ireland, Buenos Aires Municipal Autodromo in Argentina, Opatija in modern-day Croatia and Goiania in Brazil. Carruthers's ride in the 1969 Yugoslav Grand Prix was perhaps the most dramatic of these title clinchers, for the nature and condition of the seaside Opatija public-road circuit, and the knife-edge situation with three riders all needing to win the race to be champion.

Carruthers would later be part of Australia's long-term presence on the other side of the pit wall, as crew chiefs, mechanics and suspension technicians. Based in California since 1971, Carruthers tutored Kenny Roberts in tarmac riding and then brought him to the World Championships in 1978.

In the 32 seasons from then until 2009, the premier-class champion rider had an Australian crew chief 20 times — a 63 per cent success rate from Carruthers, Jeremy Burgess and the late Warren Willing.

Beyond the rider and technicians, the Australian legacy in Grand Prix racing includes a diversity of characters, a rich private-entrant tradition on the

Continental Circus, milestone moments for several manufacturers, and contributions to some innovative if not always successful machines.

In terms of characters, a script writer might have struggled to invent 1964 Finnish 500 Grand Prix winner and World Championship runner-up Jack Ahearn, 1969 500 Honda twin special builder/rider Terry Dennehy or wildcard 2006 Valencia MotoGP winner Troy Bayliss.

Few can match the gritty longevity of stalwart private riders Jack Findlay, John Dodds and Anthony West, Grand Prix winners all. Findlay returned to the Grand Prix paddock in 1992 as the inaugural FIM Technical Director. At the turn of the millennium West was part of the only Australian-formed team in the Grand Prix — Shell Advance Honda.

But think also of some lasting images: the superb natural talent of Gregg Hansford in the late 1970s, Garry McCoy, a speedway-schooled rider whose effortless power slides in 2000 prompted Rossi to say he would buy tickets to watch, and Stoner, described at his peak as perhaps the fastest rider ever and a six-time consecutive winner at Phillip Island.

What of riders who personified determination? Gardner as Australia's first 500 World Champion helped secure national free-to-air television coverage and a World Championship round at a circuit many current riders rate in their top two or three. And Doohan, who fought back from a horror injury to dominate rivals on track, winning 54 Grands Prix and two of his five titles by 143 points. Only Rossi and Giacomo Agostini have won more races in the premier class.

Historic footnotes run through this Australian story: Tom Phillis was the first to win a Grand Prix on a Japanese machine, Barry Smith was Derbi's first winner, and Dodds recorded Aermacchi's maiden win on a fog-shrouded Nürburgring in 1970. Carruthers won the 250 Grand Prix the same day, so former domestic rivals logged a rare double on privately entered machines. Carruthers had the previous year been the last to win the 250 crown on a four-stroke machine.

Jack Findlay was the first rider to win a 500 Grand Prix on a two-stroke machine (a largely self-prepared Suzuki), and Stoner brought Ducati its breakthrough Grand Prix championship.

What has underscored this success, in championships where for the first 40 years every event was an away game? A country with space to ride and outward-looking, adventurous young men. An ethos in sports as varied as football, golf, tennis and swimming of competitors who work hard, have a good competitive attitude and a strong mentality.

Add to that a long tradition in the arts as well as sport of heading halfway around the world to seek greater challenge. Entertainer Barry Humphries spoke of

LEFT The first Australian Motorcycle Grand Prix was held in 1989 at Phillip Island.

BELOW After a battle royal, Wayne Gardner had to be the rider to win that first Australian Grand Prix of 1989.

the desire "to prove oneself in the white heat of competition".

For many Australian internationals of the 1950s and 1960s — and there were more than 70 across two decades — the lure of Europe was paid, week-to-week racing. The potential to do what they loved every weekend from April to September, perhaps travelling with a good mate or a new bride and, for the first time in their careers, owning two new racing machines.

If it meant two years' toil to save the cost of new machines, the boat fare and a small cash 'float' to join the Continental Circus, so be it.

The tradition of selling virtually everything you owned to try your hand on the other side of the world applied to Tom and Betty Phillis in 1958, and Casey Stoner's family in 2000, when he was 14.

Most Australians heading to Europe in the first two decades of the World Championships had ridden their domestic careers on roadster-based specials and perhaps second-hand racers that they had maintained, learning vital preparation lessons along the way. Findlay left Melbourne in 1958 never having won a national-level race. Of the six Australian World Champions, only Carruthers had won a national title before heading overseas. He said that success meant he arrived in Europe with a reputation and so competitors were less likely to share information.

Private entrant was a noble calling and the successful ones, like Bob Brown and Keith Campbell, could head home for the southern summer and not have to work

ABOVE The Aussie duo of Mick Doohan and crew chief Jerry Burgess dominated the 500cc class in the nineties.

RIGHT The tide of change: Mick Doohan leads Honda team-mate Wayne Gardner in Hungary in 1990 to win his first Grand Prix.

in the off season. To be highest-placed private entrant in the 500cc class was a badge of honour for Brown, Ahearn and Findlay.

However, Australia's involvement in international road racing and its history of domestic road racing are even older, having both passed the century mark. Les Bailey competed in the 1912 Isle of Man TT and was the first 350cc finisher in that year's International Cup at Le Mans. The Australian TT and Grand Prix both date from 1914–15. In 1930, Arthur Simcock recorded the nation's first success in a European classic, winning the Dutch 350 TT on a factory AJS.

The country sent an official team to the 1949 Isle of Man TT, the opening round of the first championship season. It has since been represented in every premier-class championship bar 1982 and had riders 'in the points' in all except four.

When Ken Kavanagh won the 1952 Ulster 350 Grand Prix for Norton, only four nations had claimed a classic victory in solos or sidecars — Britain, Italy, Ireland and Germany. Sixty years ago, when Keith Campbell became World Champion, the previous champions had all come from Austria, England, Germany or Italy.

ABOVE Garry McCoy lit up Grand Prix racing with his tyre-smoking, sliding style that brought him three 500cc victories in 2000.

BELOW Aussie crew chief Warren Willing was the mastermind behind Kenny Roberts Jr's 500cc world title in 2000.

ABOVE Valentino Rossi and Sete Gibernau fight it out at the magnificent Phillip Island in 2004 with the Bass Strait providing a dream background.

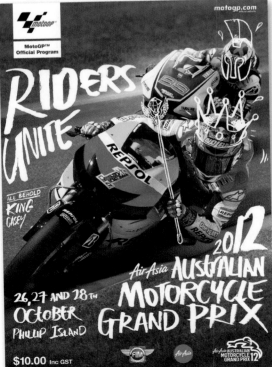

RIGHT Casey Stoner's last Grand Prix victory came at Phillip Island in 2012.

"The Australians had the first hurdle covered by coming over," said seven-time champion John Surtees. "Those who came showed they had the ambition to succeed." And having travelled 18,000 kilometres, typically spending six weeks on a ship, they showed resilience, a resistance to quitting easily and a reluctance to accept second place.

As 13-times title-winning crew chief Jeremy Burgess described it: "You really go there to put in the extra effort to win. The trip home is a lot better if you've won than if you're fourth or fifth."

Kenny Roberts as a team owner said in 1987: "Most Australians have the right attitude about working and racing. They give 120 per cent, they don't complain, they don't get homesick."

In the 1980s, Australian riders, along with Americans, were the riders factories hired to race 500s, as they had been brought up travelling sideways on dirt tracks. Journalist Mat Oxley noted, "This was racing's only era when regional riding talent, rather than regional industry and finance, made the difference."

In fact, riders like Gardner, who started riding on mini-bikes, were the latest example of a dirt-

LEFT Phillip Island rightly honoured Casey Stoner by naming Turn Three after the double MotoGP World Champion.

BELOW Jack Miller continued the Australian tradition after his wet-weather MotoGP win at Assen in 2016.

track lineage stretching back to 1930s, as well as a founding role in speedway. Where the United States had booming V-twins racing on county fairgrounds, Australia's under-recognized dirt-track tradition was created on bush or suburban-fringe circuits with both right-hand and left-hand corners, and peppered with home-built 500 specials.

For racing enthusiasts in Australia, reflecting on the last 25 years means a period when the country has had its own Grand Prix throughout and had two superstar riders in Doohan and Stoner. In 1992 we seemed blessed, with a championship round and two circuits capable of hosting a Grand Prix, while Doohan and Gardner held both seats in the works Honda team. When Gardner sustained a broken leg at Suzuka in 1992, a third Australian, Daryl Beattie, rode in his place.

Ten years earlier there had been no Australian riders in the 500 World Championship and a few years later the country's premier race meeting was under threat, due to crowd disturbances. But progress was swift from there, in no small measure thanks to Wayne Gardner's success and the vision of inaugural Australian Grand Prix promoter Bob Barnard.

CHAPTER 18
GERMANY
TIMES OF CHANGE
BY GÜNTHER WIESINGER

Germany has a unique history in motorcycle racing, especially given that the country was split into two nations after the Second World War — West Germany (Federal Republic of Germany) and East Germany (the German Democratic Republic) — until the fall of the Berlin Wall brought reunification in 1990. The division between capitalist West and communist East, including the abandonment of freedom of travel between them, brought about many peculiarities, not only in daily life but also for motorcycle racing.

East Germany had a big setback in 1961, the year the Berlin Wall was built. At that time MZ factory rider Ernst Degner, an East German citizen and also a skilled engineer, was leading the 125cc World Championship. In the lead-up to the Swedish GP in Kristianstad, Degner got a West German friend to smuggle his wife and children into the trunk of an American car and flee from East Berlin to the west. Only when he knew his family was safe in West Germany did he make the journey to Sweden. There he met Suzuki team manager Jimmy Matsumiya and handed over a bag containing all sorts of material about high-performance two-stroke technology as developed by brilliant MZ engineer Walter Kaaden; it has even been reported that Degner provided Suzuki with a complete MZ bike built from spare parts.

So it was that Degner got a Suzuki contract for

RIGHT The first German Grand Prix was held at the Solitude circuit near Stuttgart in 1952 and the 500cc race was won by Reg Armstrong on a Norton.

FAR RIGHT Hockenheim staged its first German Grand Prix in 1957.

1962 and helped to develop new 125cc and 50cc Suzuki engines. Degner duly won the 50cc World Championship in 1962 and Suzuki, using its highly developed MZ technology, went on to dominate the smaller categories, winning one title after another. Eventually, from 1976 onwards, titles in the 500cc category followed, for riders such as Barry Sheene, Marco Lucchinelli, Franco Uncini, Kevin Schwantz and Kenny Roberts Jr.

After this scandal, the MZ factory team was forbidden by the state to take part in foreign Grands Prix and Degner, needless to say, was considered a traitor. However, a World Championship Grand Prix continued in East Germany until 1972, held on the 8.7-kilometre street circuit at the Sachsenring in Hohenstein-Ernstthal.

West Germany's Dieter Braun was the 125cc World Champion of 1970 on a Suzuki and moved up to the 250cc category with Yamaha for 1971. That year the East German regime did everything it could to complicate Braun's participation in the 250cc Grand Prix at the Sachsenring, held mid-season, but the Yamaha rider was well placed in the points standings and was determined to take part in the race by whatever means required — and he won it. The post-race atmosphere was particularly sinister.

"The Stasi [secret police] had known from 1969 that there was a danger of me winning," Braun remembers. "So they installed the public-address loudspeakers in such a way that they could be switched off around the track if needed. After the race the

LEFT Ernst Degner brought much success to MZ before defecting to Suzuki.

Deutschland-Lied anthem was heard only on the main straight as the FIM steward was watching there and FIM rules stated that the national anthem of the GP winner had to be played."

The *Volkspolizei* (the national police force) attended in large numbers, many of them accompanied by

BELOW Ernst Degner lines up his MZ (8) on the 125cc 1959 Dutch TT grid alongside Mike Hailwood (4).

ABOVE Ernst Degner
brought Suzuki its first
Grand Prix win and 50cc
world title in 1962.

SACHSEN RING

Weltmeisterschaftslauf
für Motorräder
Großer Preis der
Deutschen
Demokratischen Republik
9. bis 11. Juli 1971

Veranstalter: Allgemeiner Deutscher Motorsportverband der DDR

068141

RIGHT The 1971 East
German Grand Prix at the
Sachsenring that caused so
much controversy.

dogs, such was the regime's determination not to allow
any celebrations to get out of hand. "The fans were
going crazy behind the fences," recalls photographer
Fritz Glänzel, who was at the race. "It was frightening.
Everyone was going mad."

Somewhat ironically, a victory for a German rider
meant the end for the Sachsenring's Grand Prix. The East
German authorities did not want to allow the repressed
population to witness any more wins by 'capitalist' riders.

"My Sachsenring victory was a brilliant result," adds
Braun. "After my 125cc title on the former Anscheidt-
Suzuki in 1970, Toni Mang and Sepp Schlögel came in
to be my mechanics in Grand Prix racing, so all my bikes
were much better prepared in 1971. I was able to fight
the best riders in the world at the Sachsenring and win
against them, against Read, Gould, Saarinen, Sheene
and Mortimer. My competitors were all — at least
to a certain degree — factory-supported and I was a
privateer… But I still managed to achieve my first 250cc
GP win."

The East German authorities even intended to
disqualify Braun after his win for crossing a white line
marking the edge of the track.

"That would have been against the FIM rules," Braun explains. "The rules state that if you cross the white line on the inside to shorten the track and gain an advantage, you can be disqualified. But I didn't shorten on the inside coming down the hill — this wouldn't have been possible. I simply overtook a backmarker on the outside. The last one and a half metres of the track were dirty, with dust and rubber. There it was much more slippery than on the racing line, which I had to leave due to this backmarker. I couldn't have waited until after the corner, as my competitors were following closely — that's why I came through on the slippery part of the road.

"That was quite a moment, but this corner luckily had some banking so the bike stabilized itself again at around 240km/h. That was a scary moment. The East German authorities were briefly excited and thought: 'Now he has crashed.' The FIM steward later assured me that no rider could be disqualified for riding over the white line in the way I did."

When the huge crowd started to sing the *Deutschland-Lied*, even the hardened racer Braun became emotional.

ABOVE Dieter Braun on the way to his first 250cc Grand Prix win, in East Germany at the Sachsenring.

BELOW Glum faces on the 1971 Sachsenring 250cc podium with winner Dieter Braun (centre) flanked by Rodney Gould (left) and Phil Read.

"That was amazing. Even Rodney Gould and Phil Read were overwhelmed. The passion of the fans, everyone could feel it. Almost 280,000 people cheered in support and my fans had banners with them."

Braun, a 14-time Grand Prix winner, was also one of the pioneers of rider safety and, like Sheene and others, helped to ban the dangerous street-racing circuits. He also acknowledges that Grand Prix motorcycle racing has improved hugely since Dorna took over.

"The work of Dorna has had a very positive impact," Braun states. "For 20 years nothing was done or improved and officials did not have any interest in safety. When I said something about the safety and brought in some ideas, I only got the answer, 'We have been riding here like this for 20 years' — and that was it. For how long did we have to fight against the World Championship status of the Tourist Trophy and other dangerous street circuits? GP circuits nowadays are much safer, you can't argue about that. Now the riders have a spokesman who was active himself for many years and he was very good, a 500cc World Champion — Franco Uncini. That is a big advantage."

Since 1949 many German motorcycle manufacturers

ABOVE Edmund Czihak was the surprise winner of the 1974 West German 500cc Grand Prix when the top riders boycotted the race at the Nürburgring on safety grounds.

BELOW Toni Mang in action at the 1981 250cc French Grand Prix — he dominated the 250cc and 350cc classes with both Kawasaki and Honda.

LEFT & BELOW On a limited budget Dirk Raudies won the 1993 125cc World Championship.

have taken part in the World Championship, such as DKW, NSU, Horex, BMW, Zündapp, Maico — and many more. Today, however, only Kalex participates.

The first German Grand Prix was held in 1952 at the Solitude circuit close to Stuttgart. In addition the Schottenring was also the scene of Grand Prix racing, before the permanent race tracks of Hockenheimring and Nürburgring featured on the calendar. In 1998 the motorcycle World Championship returned to the shortened 3.5-kilometre Sachsenring.

Since 1949 German riders have amassed 190 Grand Prix wins, but only one has been in the premier class, when Edmund Czihak won at the Nürburgring in 1974. But this win had something of a blemish, as only seven riders took part and they were all German, as the rest of the regular runners boycotted the event due to safety concerns. For the same reason, the other races that weekend in solo categories went to German underdogs as well: Ingo Emmerich (50cc), Fritz Reitmaier (125cc) and Helmut Kassner (250cc and 350cc).

The most successful German rider ever is Anton 'Toni' Mang, with 42 Grand Prix wins in the period 1976–1988 and five world titles, four of them for Kawasaki in the years 1980–1982 and a fifth riding a Honda in 1987. Since Mang's triumphs, only Dirk Raudies (125cc/1993), Stefan Bradl (Moto2/2011) and Sandro Cortese (Moto3/2012) have added to Germany's list of World Champions. Ralf Waldmann, meanwhile, achieved a unique record of notching up 20 GP wins without becoming a World Champion.

The aforementioned Raudies was riding at the time the World Championship was taken over from the FIM by Dorna. In 1989 he was already featuring in the top six in the 125cc class and he had his most successful years in the post-Dorna era, achieving a total of 23 podiums.

Almost unbelievably, in the 1993 season when Raudies won his 125cc world title, he was the owner of his team. The total team budget for the whole season was the equivalent of around €150,000 and his main sponsor provided €13,000 of that. He only had one mechanic, his brother-in-law, and during FP1 on Fridays he used old tyres from the previous Grand Prix.

"At that time I was very happy that Dorna and FIM made their agreement and there was no breakaway series," Raudies remembers. "As a team owner I supported the arrival of Dorna. Prior to Dorna I would get 5,000 Swiss Francs for a GP win — and that was it. With Dorna the income quadrupled at least, as we got starting money, prize money, TV money and a subsidy for expenses. That was really important for small teams and we could plan our budgets much better. We knew that even with less success we would have a certain fixed income."

For many, the pre-Dorna era is just a distant memory. Before 1992, organizers decided which teams and riders would participate each weekend and how many categories would race — from 50cc, 125cc, 250cc, 350cc and 500cc to sidecars — depending on the time schedule. Sometimes even World

ABOVE & RIGHT Stefan Bradl went one better than his father Helmut and won the 2011 Moto2 world title.

Championship leaders or title favourites were not allowed to start, such as Kawasaki factory rider Gregg Hansford at Jarama in the 250cc race in 1979.

There was no permanent race direction and sometimes medical aid was in short supply, as at Rijeka in 1990, when Reinhold Roth suffered serious injury. There were also big mistakes by race direction, such as at Spa-Francorchamps in 1989 when the 500cc race was started three times, contrary to FIM rules. Sometimes there were also strikes, as in 1974 at the Nürburgring, 1977 at the Salzburgring, 1979 at Spa-Francorchamps and 1989 at Misano.

During the past 25 years the FIM Road Racing World Championship has entered a new era. The FIM has become more professional, with some obstinate traditionalists getting removed thanks to Vito Ippolito, whose father discovered Johnny Cecotto and brought Grand Prix racing to Venezuela.

The big factories returned to MotoGP as racing switched to four-strokes, which was better for marketing and technical development. Furthermore, new sponsors have come in and the numbers of spectators have increased.

ABOVE & BELOW German rider Sandro Cortese was the first Moto3 World Champion in 2012 after a tremendous battle with Luis Salom.

CHAPTER 19
FRANCE
ALLEZ LES BLEUS
BY THOMAS BAUJARD

Since the start of the World Championship in 1949, a lot has happened in France. From the first dangerous road circuits and amateur racers to today's top professional athletes riding on safe but physically demanding tracks, a mesmerising journey has taken place.

"The first thing to know is that in the fifties there was not a French Grand Prix every year," explains Jacques Bussillet, editor of the leading motorcycle magazine *Moto Journal* and Grand Prix reporter from the early seventies to the early eighties. "The very first Grand Prix de France took place on 14 July 1951 at Albi, close to Toulouse, in the south of France. After that, there was

BELOW Pierre Monneret won the 500cc race at his home Grand Prix at Reims in 1954.

one at Rouen (1953), two at Reims (1954 and 1955) and one at the Charade track near Clermont-Ferrand (1959).

"Short of funds, the organisers of these events did not want to run races for all the available classes. Sometimes, as at Rouen and Reims, it was three classes only: 250cc, 350cc and 500cc. This was the minimum allowed by the Fédération Internationale de Motocyclisme (FIM).

"Then the French Grand Prix went to Clermont-Ferrand every year from 1960 to 1967, except for one visit to Rouen, in 1965. In 1969 it was held at Le Mans for the first time, on the Bugatti circuit. That day all six leading racers in the 125cc class suffered mechanical problems, and the seventh fastest happened to be Frenchman Jean Auréal, who won the race on a Yamaha!

"The riders loved the Charade track: eight kilometres with all types of corners and changes of elevation. But the lack of run-off made it extremely dangerous and the organization was a disaster. At the beginning of the 1960s, the situation was not helped by changeable weather. Thick fog led to the cancellation of all but one of the races in 1963 and only the 50cc field got away.

"Until the start of the 1970s, the French Federation awarded the Grand Prix to different circuits each year as an incentive for the organizers, giving them the possibility to earn more money after having a hard time with less prestigious races in previous years. That caused a lot of trouble at Clermont-Ferrand in 1974 when the riders asked why they were still racing there, given that the safer Paul Ricard now existed and had hosted the Grand Prix for the first time the previous year.

"In these first two decades of the World Championship, there were few French riders, but there were occasional good moments. Pierre Monneret won both the 350cc and 500cc races at Reims in 1954 on his factory AJS and Gilera, although on that day Tourist Trophy practice had already started on the

GRAND PRIX DE FRANCE
MOTOCYCLISTE
ALBI

15 JUILLET 1951

PROGRAMME OFFICIEL   PRIX : 100 fr.

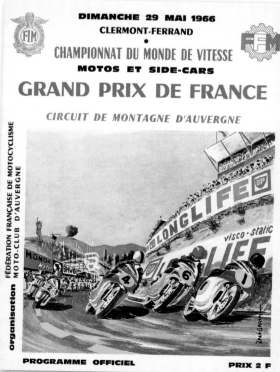

DIMANCHE 29 MAI 1966
CLERMONT-FERRAND
•
CHAMPIONNAT DU MONDE DE VITESSE
MOTOS ET SIDE-CARS
GRAND PRIX DE FRANCE
CIRCUIT DE MONTAGNE D'AUVERGNE

organisation FÉDÉRATION FRANÇAISE DE MOTOCYCLISME
MOTO-CLUB D'AUVERGNE

PROGRAMME OFFICIEL   PRIX 2 F

ABOVE A 1964 Grand Prix start at Clermont-Ferrand, the challenging circuit in France's Massif Central.

FAR LEFT The first French Grand Prix was staged in 1951 at Albi in south-west France.

LEFT Between 1959 and 1974 the French Grand Prix was held at Clermont-Ferrand 10 times.

PROGRAMME PRIX 5F
28·29·30 MARS 1975
CIRCUIT PAUL RICARD

GRAND PRIX DE FRANCE
MOTO
CHAMPIONNAT DU MONDE

Isle of Man and factory squads were missing. At the end of the fifties only eight French riders participated in their home Grand Prix, including Jacques Collot and Jacques Insermini in the 500cc class and sidecar racer Joseph Duhem.

Nanou Findlay, the French girlfriend of Australian top privateer racer Jack Findlay, now aged 89 and living in Nice, explains her Charade experience: "The paddock was a sloping field in the countryside. That's about it. It was real mayhem when it rained. The wheels of the bikes got completely covered with mud and we had to clean them before they went on the track. The only water in the paddock was from a hose lying on the ground. I acted as an interpreter to translate all the complaints from the foreign racers to the organizer, Monsieur Cornet, and got rudely told off by his wife, a loud-mouthed bartender!"

Everything changed in 1970 with the construction of the Paul Ricard track close to Toulon. "Paul Ricard was the most modern race track on the planet," says Jacques Bussillet. "It was also a beautiful and really broad, safe circuit with a proper paddock that was easy to get to thanks to a tunnel under the track. At

Clermont-Ferrand, as soon as the first practice started, paddock access was denied!

"An FIM rule stated that a circuit had to stage an international race before hosting a Grand Prix. That happened in 1970, but then Paul Ricard had to wait until 22 April 1973 for its first Grand Prix. It was a phenomenal success, capped with two Jarno Saarinen victories. As venues were still being alternated, Paul Ricard hosted the Grand Prix only twice more that decade, in 1975 and 1977.

"In this period French riders started to score points and gradually they got the opportunity to win their home race. The first French winner at the French Grand Prix in the seventies was sidecar racer Alain Michel at Paul Ricard in 1977. A summit was reached two years later, at Le Mans in 1979, when Guy Bertin won the 125cc class on a French Motobecane — sponsored by Pernod! — and then Patrick Fernandez won the 350cc event, after the retirement of compatriot Eric Saul, who led three-quarters of the race. Given the lack of success of French racers in the previous 30 years, Monneret, Auréal and Michel apart, this outcome on one weekend was phenomenal.

ABOVE Patrick Fernandez (centre) celebrates his 350cc victory at Le Mans in 1979 with Walter Villa and Roland Freymond.

BELOW Watch the tree: 250cc World Champion Jean-Louis Tournadre in action at Imatra in Finland in 1982.

"From 1970, prominent radio stations such as Europe 1 and RTL, and established newspapers such as *France Soir*, all had reporters at the French Grand Prix, and the races were televised. France was also providing many sponsors, with Giacomo Agostini wearing French leathers and Phil Read having a contract with Elf. All this helped to nurture French riders.

"Sadly, by the end of that decade motorcycling in general was starting to lose its mainstream appeal. Racing-wise, only one importer, Yamaha Motor France, kept fighting for its racers with a proper team. France was one of the first countries where the core motorcycle audience started to lose interest in racing. For the general public, bikes were no longer quite so fashionable."

On a tragic note, four top-class French racers were killed in the space of mere months in 1980 and 1981. Olivier Chevallier, younger brother of technician Alain Chevallier, died after falling off in the fast Verrerie Esses at Paul Ricard on the fifth lap of the 250cc race at the *Moto Journal* 200 event on 6 April 1980; Olivier was remarkable not only for his talent but also his unparalleled skill in securing sponsorship. On 10 August, 750cc champion Patrick Pons collided with Michel Rougerie at Silverstone, and died two days afterwards. On 8 November, Christian Léon, Grand Prix racer until 1975 and then endurance factory rider, hit a wall on the notoriously dangerous Suzuki road course in Ryuyo and died shortly afterwards. The following year, on 31 May, Michel Rougerie, 250cc World Championship runner-up

ABOVE Christian Sarron celebrates his 250cc world title of 1984.

RIGHT Christian Sarron leads Eddie Lawson to become the first French premier-class race winner for 31 years with victory at Hockenheim in 1985.

in 1975, fell on the second lap of the 350cc Yugoslav Grand Prix in Rijeka and was hit by his friend and team-mate Roger Sibille.

"I started as a GP reporter in 1982," explains Bruno Gillet, who today remains a freelance journalist for *Moto Journal* and *GP+*. "That year, the unknown privateer racer Jean-Louis Tournadre became World Champion in the intermediate class, a real feat. But his career then dwindled: he didn't score a single point the following year, so gave up racing and became an engineer.

"In 1982, Honda came back to racing with a 500cc three-cylinder two-stroke and three riders: Freddie Spencer, whom we didn't know, Marco Lucchinelli, who had just won the 500cc title, and the Japanese rider Takazumi Katayama. Nogaro was the third Grand Prix of the season, but the riders went on strike, once more because of safety issues."

After that, Le Mans and Paul Ricard alternated in hosting the French Grand Prix, with the one exception of Magny Cours in 1992, until the closure of Paul Ricard as a public venue in 1999 and its transformation by Bernie Ecclestone into a Formula One testing facility. Since then the race has always been held at Le Mans.

"I got lucky because of all the French riders I got to witness the greatest of all was Christian Sarron," testifies Bruno. "Even if Johann Zarco has overtaken him in terms of world titles, Christian is the one who shone most in the class of kings, and at a time when competition was fierce with riders like Schwantz, Lawson, Gardner and Rainey. Riding Yamahas between 1985 and 1989, Christian scored 18 rostrum finishes, with one victory, in the 1985 West German Grand Prix, three second places and 14 thirds. He won the 250cc World Championship title in 1984 and was runner-up the year before. In the 500 class he didn't have the best bike or the best tyres.

"Raymond Roche was good as well with five runner-up placings in 500cc races despite arm-pump problems in 1984 and 1985, and he was third in the points standings in 1984 on a Honda.

"It was not only the French riders that were pushing the sport forward but also engineers, none more so than the brilliant Serge Rosset. He produced the revolutionary Elf-Honda with a self-supported engine and magnesium forks. British rider Ron Haslam took two successive podium finishes and finished fourth in the 1987 500cc World Championship on a machine that was way ahead of its time.

"Dominique Sarron, Christian's younger brother, snatched four victories and eight pole positions between 1986 and 1988 in the intermediate class on his factory NSR Honda.

"After that, Jean-Philippe Ruggia came along at the end of the eighties. He was hugely talented, earning three 250 victories and nine podiums in total, but he was also very stubborn and didn't want to evolve in any way at all, which ruined his career. With data acquisition just beginning at this time, he dubbed it 'the sneak' and didn't listen to anyone. When he complained about a lack of top speed, his engineers replied that

BELOW The start of the Italian Grand Prix at Misano in 1990, the year France's Alain Michel (3) became sidecar World Champion, here in company with multiple World Champions Steve Webster (1), Rolf Biland (4) and Egbert Streuer (2).

RIGHT Serge Rosset with rider Ron Haslam and a model of the unique Elf-Honda.

BELOW Olivier Jacque in action on the Yamaha after moving on to the MotoGP class following his 250cc world title of 2000.

above 14,000rpm there wasn't much power left in a two-stroke engine, but he still took it up to 16,000rpm! When downshifting, he revved so high that the reed valves got swallowed up by the engine, something that engineers could never replicate on their test bench. Despite that, he got good 250cc Yamahas at Sonauto, a factory Honda NSR250 at Tech3, and factory Aprilias with team-mate Max Biaggi and Carlo Pernat as team manager.

"Olivier Jacque was mentally one of the strongest French riders ever. The downside to this was that he crashed a lot. He became World Champion in 2000 on the relatively underpowered Yamaha YZR 250 with Tech3, beating his team-mate Shinya Nakano by a mere 0.014 second to clinch the title on the last lap of the last Grand Prix of the season at Phillip Island. It was the closest championship-winning margin in the history of the sport.

"Then along came double Moto2 Champion Johann Zarco, who is somehow the modern synthesis of several French riders of the past. Maybe Zarco doesn't quite have Jacque's nerves of steel, but he has the talent, dedication, work ethic and outstanding physical qualities needed to win. This blend of skills impressed Hervé Poncharal, boss of the French Tech3 team, enough to enrol Zarco as a rookie in his MotoGP squad."

Despite the relatively low awareness of MotoGP as a sport for the mainstream public in France, the country has another ace up its MotoGP sleeve: the French Grand Prix at Le Mans.

"Claude Michy, the promoter, is the last private entity left in the Grand Prix organization business," explains Bruno Gillet. "Carmelo Ezpeleta, Dorna's boss, admires him for his endeavour, because Claude is the only one not to rely on public funds to set up his Grand Prix, in a country where legal aspects are a real nightmare. Despite all these burdens, the Grand Prix at Le Mans is a success year after year, and it has become the fourth biggest attendance of the season, with more than 100,000 people on race day."

Michy can also count on Dorna to establish a fair set of rules and a truly competitive championship in all three classes to spice up the show. Even if the track is less challenging than 30 years ago, with the Chemin aux Bœufs flat-out left replaced by a chicane, Michy receives the accolade of Valentino Rossi himself: "A great Grand Prix, it is like racing between two huge rows of spectators all around the lap!"

With an experienced MotoGP team like Tech3, a promising rider like Johann Zarco and a prime arena to celebrate him like Le Mans, there is no reason why the French MotoGP future should not be bright. In other words: *"Allez les Bleus!"*

ABOVE & BELOW The new generation – the impressive Johann Zarco won two Moto2 world titles before switching to MotoGP.

PART 5

THE TECHNICAL STORY

Ducati mechanics in action on Andrea
Dovisioso's bike in Austin, Texas, in 2016.

CHAPTER 20
FOUR-TWO-FOUR
BY KEVIN CAMERON

When Dorna assumed management of FIM GP racing in 1992, it was an established and functioning series. Twenty-five years before, huge crowds had been happy to see Giacomo Agostini win 500cc GPs by six minutes over a thundering herd of vintage Nortons. Since then, the coming of television had greatly raised the expected standard of excitement. Bernie Ecclestone, in demonstrating that F1 could reach that standard, showed that motorsport could be a profitable TV-based entertainment business — not just old gentlemen in blue blazers, guarding a hundred years of motoring tradition.

Such a business required a stable population of teams, but the history of motorcycle GP racing was anything but. Instead, teams and their strength waxed and waned with motorcycling's importance as transportation. Bike sales soared after the Second World War, but crashed when car production resumed. British GP teams withdrew after 1954, German teams a year later, and most Italian teams two years after that, leaving mainly MV Agusta and the single-cylinder privateers. In the 1960s came the Japanese, raising the GPs to unprecedented heights as Honda, Yamaha, and Suzuki made their names in racing. A sudden stop came at the end of 1967, when Honda withdrew and the others soon followed.

RIGHT The two-stroke Honda NSR dominated the nineties with Mick Doohan and Álex Crivillé.

For a time, MV was virtually the sole factory involved, and privateers rode mainly Japanese production racers in the 125, 250 and 350 classes. The sudden 1972 success of US 750 road racing showed Japan racing's continuing value in a time when motorcycles had evolved into sport and leisure goods. As a result, Yamaha and Suzuki entered 500cc GP racing, bringing new life and value to that class just as MV left the scene.

Two-strokes began their long dominance of all GP classes in 1975. This was ultimately progressive, for the steep rise of horsepower in the premier class forced development of valuable new chassis, suspension and tyre technologies that would soon benefit all of motorcycling.

During Dorna's era of stewardship of 500cc racing from 1992 to 2001, they managed a status quo, adopting low-lead fuel in the early 1990s, then adopting no-lead in 1998, in conformity with society as a whole.

PROBLEMS

Two-strokes, despite their high power and light weight, had no future. National vehicle emissions laws forbade their production for street and highway, eliminating any

new-manufacturer motivation to develop two-strokes. This limited the series to the makers already present — Honda, Yamaha, Suzuki and Aprilia. What if Honda withdrew, as they had at the end of 1967? What new team would dare challenge Mick Doohan's five championships in a row on Honda?

Despite being exciting to watch, 500cc two-strokes and their lap times had stagnated. Technologies had been developed to soften the sudden 'hit' of two-stroke torque, but they still had to be ridden defensively. Riders turned their bikes early, then lifted up to put down enough tyre footprint to take the hit, hoping not to high-side on corner exit. Two-stroke 500s remained so difficult to ride that few men could reach the front — so grids lacked depth of talent.

With four-stroke power, these objections disappeared. New manufacturers without their own two-stroke technologies, such as Ducati and BMW, could draw upon widely available four-stroke technology, knowing that anything learned on the track could have direct application to production four-strokes. With more controllable torque, four-strokes could be ridden well by a larger number of riders, creating

ABOVE Honda led the four-stroke revolution with the RC211V, which brought Valentino Rossi the world title in 2002.

ABOVE The new 800s line up at the start of the 2007 season before the opening Grand Prix in Qatar.

closer competition and raising public interest. Sito Pons, running a Honda team, relayed to Dorna the message that "the constructors wanted a change to four-strokes". Discussion with the manufacturers — including Ducati and Aprilia — followed.

Four-strokes it would be, but at what displacement? Continuing at 500cc would have been an anti-climax, since 750 Superbikes (then still under independent Flammini management) would be faster. The 750 and 1,000 capacities already appeared to 'belong' to other series. In the marketplace, 1,000cc sportbikes were fast becoming the most sought-after. There was discussion of something around 835cc but, in the end, the stone began to move when Mick Doohan in 1996 said to Dorna's Carmelo Ezpeleta, "Just give us a litre and we'll all be sideways." A litre's displacement (990cc was the chosen figure) would ensure that the new bikes decisively eclipsed the 500s and their lap records.

LEARNING

At first, Honda's Yasuo Ikenoya stated that their MotoGP bike would use no exotic technologies and require no service techniques beyond those found in

Superbike. This was a reasonable expectation, as the bigger the engine, the lower the level of tune required to produce good performance. But very quickly Yamaha discovered that their first design, which was smaller than the full 990 displacement and used a Superbike-style chain cam drive and carburettors, needed rapid upgrades to be competitive. After two years, 500cc two-strokes were no longer admitted to the class.

There were other surprises. The riders were not all sideways because tyre development had served the needs of riders graduating from the 125 and 250 classes, where relative lack of acceleration required a corner-speed style that was dependent upon side grip. Because the new four-strokes did not have the two-stroke 'torque hit', riders could begin feeding power at high corner-lean angle. This had two effects. First, lap times again dropped, less because of increased power than because four-strokes could accelerate earlier. And second, a new 'MotoGP corner style' emerged, with much higher apex speeds.

In the era of Kenny Roberts, the much-admired 'point-and-shoot' riding style had produced exciting sideways cowboy riding, so tyres had developed to take the abuse of sliding rather than maximize grip. The last decade of the 500s reversed this, so the tyres MotoGP inherited delivered strong grip but could not last race distance if ridden sideways — as tyre smokers like Garry McCoy would soon discover.

There was a new problem: braking instability. The combination of the strong engine braking of such large four-stroke engines (two-strokes had no engine braking at all) with the rapid deceleration possible with carbon brakes caused rear tyres to slide, then oscillate from side to side, sometimes causing crashes. Slipper clutches, effective in Superbike, were not enough in MotoGP. A new technology — the 'throttle kicker', borrowed from F1 — was used to feed in just enough engine power during braking to cancel any desired amount of engine braking.

With high-grip tyres and the new MotoGP riding style driving corner speeds higher, some riders — Valentino Rossi foremost among them — said run-off areas were becoming marginal. As has often happened in motorsport in the past, a chorus of "too fast" could be heard. The mysterious MSMA (Motor Sports Manufacturers' Association) articulated this differently, seeking to reduce displacement to 800cc "because it was more of a technical challenge".

The consequences of technology are not knowable in advance, so the 800cc era must be seen as a management learning experience. Top computer experts of 1972 said personal computers could never happen, but today the smartphone in your hand makes

mainframes of 1972 look stupid. In the first 800cc test, run after Valencia at the end of 2006, the new Ducati 800 showed that smaller did not mean slower. The new focus of racing was on fully exploiting tyre grip while at high motorcycle lean angle

The US Apollo moon landings had forced digital flight-control technology into existence. It spread naturally to aircraft, then implemented control strategies in Formula One, and then in production cars. Compared with cars, motorcycles have very limited tyre grip, so digital control concepts became natural partners with riders in the tricky, fast-changing problem of matching engine torque to available tyre grip. MotoGP led the electronics revolution in motorcycling, now to be found in any showroom.

The product that racing sells to the public is the excitement of close, unpredictable competition among equals, but motorcycle manufacturers have completely different goals — to make their brand appear invincible and to develop new technologies. For Honda, Mick Doohan's five-year dominance was perfect, but for the success of racing in the entertainment marketplace it was a catastrophe.

Rules can not resolve this, for manufacturers can simply quit a series they dislike. The underlying strategy, therefore, has to be one of honey rather than vinegar. The task was to make the series so successful, so essential to all manufacturers' sales and market image (especially in the growing southern Asian and South American markets) that they must remain in it. Part of

LEFT Yamaha came out on top in the 800cc battle with Valentino Rossi taking his eighth world title in 2008.

BELOW A bit more than
just the rev counter — the
instrument panel on the
2011 Honda.

this is winning the manufacturers' trust that regulation will be fair and management intelligent.

In 2008 top riders left Michelin for Bridgestone, and for the following year MotoGP adopted the 'spec' tyre concept (previously shown to be workable by World Superbike), with Bridgestone as sole supplier.

The 800cc era brought rapid electronics development to manage traction and engine torque, especially at very high lean angles. An example was Yamaha's 'mu learning' system of 2008. Each time a traction-control system acts, it is measuring the tyre grip available at that point on the track surface. Because GPS now adds just a tiny chip to the ECU board, each traction measurement could easily be paired with its position on the track to construct a digital map of the coefficient of friction (mu) on the racing line around the track. This could then be combined with another innovation — throttle-by-wire — to allow this map to enhance acceleration off corners.

Also adopted from F1 was the concept of a 'virtual powerband'; the higher an engine's state of tune, the more traction-upsetting features its torque curve displays. Since full throttle is only a small part of each lap, throttle-by-wire can be programmed to trim the mountain tops and fill in the valleys, smoothing engine torque so that riders need less help in managing it, more fully exploiting tyre grip.

This rapid development of control software brought varied responses. Traditionalists wanted to rip out all the electronics, but that would soon have turned MotoGP into a vintage class. Riders accepted the safety aspect of electronics but wanted full control in situations where that worked better. Some critics declared that racing had become a dull procession but in fact there were now more riders in serious contention than there had ever been during the 500cc days. Here were the makings of a golden age.

The three controlling variables in horsepower are engine displacement, net stroke-averaged combustion pressure, and rpm. The first was regulated to 800cc (from 2007 to 2011) and the second limited by atmospheric pressure, fuel quality and friction to about 1,400kPa. That left rpm as the open path to power. As peak rpm rose, steel valve springs were worked so hard that they needed daily replacement, so factories now adopted pneumatic springs (except Ducati with its desmodromic valve operation), just as F1 had done. At elevated rpm, exceptional materials were required for reciprocating parts. Just as in electronics software development, this split the teams into haves and have-nots. Haves could afford valves and wristpins made of aerospace intermetallics and pistons forged from custom-made dispersion-hardened aluminium. Have-nots just went slower.

BACK TO A LITRE

One step, taken for 2010, was to limit each rider to six engines per season. For 2012 Dorna slowed the costly rpm race (then fast approaching 20,000) in two ways, first by increasing engine displacement to 1,000cc, so there would be less need for radical tuning, and second by preventing extreme F1-like bore/stroke ratios with a mandated maximum bore of 81mm (implying a minimum stroke of 48.5mm) plus a four-cylinder limit.

Why not simply (and cheaply) limit the third controlling variable — rpm? Here be politics! Honda, through their MotoGP team manager Shuhei Nakamoto, had let it be known that they absolutely opposed a rev limit or common ECU software. If these things were imposed, Honda would leave the series.

NEW CLASSES

Let's look at the second GP class created by Dorna, Moto2, which in 2010 took the place of the 250cc category. The reasons for change were clear: the 1949 FIM rules calling for 125cc, 250cc, 350cc, 500cc and sidecar machines were right for post-war Europe, when so many manufacturers produced only small-bore bikes, and when sidecars remained in wide use. Great riders such as Tarquinio Provini and Luigi Taveri could spend their entire careers in these small classes. But by the 21st century those manufacturers had disappeared, and the 125 and 250 classes that had survived the 'TV cull' of the confusing 50, 80, 350 and sidecar classes were based on the cylinders of bikes that no longer existed — the 500 two-strokes.

The purpose of smaller classes had changed. Instead of showcasing small manufacturers, the new purpose is to prepare riders for MotoGP. In past decades production racers such as Yamaha TZs had made these classes affordable, but the cost of a 250 'seat' (two bikes, spares and factory advice) had risen to nearly 1 million Euro. Technical development is fascinating but, if uncontrolled, strong teams buy speed others cannot afford. To stop this, Moto2 bikes would be driven

by identical Honda CBR600 engines built to equal power by a single agency. Because tyre wars push manufacturers to the edge of reliability, a 'spec' tyre was required, sourced from Dunlop.

At the time, it was proposed that because Moto2 chassis were unregulated, the class would unleash a flood of chassis innovation. Just as watercolourists often achieve their best results accidentally, so rule-making can have consequences other than those intended.

Chassis were offered by many constructors, but conformity rather than innovation resulted as teams settled on those chassis that gave quickest lap times and discarded the others. Racing is pragmatic.

Moto2 showed unique value in a surprising way. With so many traditional racing variables either specified or controlled, it was the riders themselves who innovated. While most competitors rode hard to stay in the lead group, a thoughtful few devised ways

ABOVE The Yamaha YZR M1 of the 1,000cc period as seen in 2013, when Jorge Lorenzo won eight Grands Prix but still finished second in the title chase.

subject to a rev limit and minimum number of engines supplied per manufacturer as tools to discourage 'tech-war'.

FILLING MOTOGP GRIDS

In MotoGP the 2011 season made it clear that full fields of 20–22 pure factory entries would not happen. Rider injuries in Australia chopped the starting field there to 14, below the contractual minimum of 15. Time for extraordinary measures! To put private teams on the grids, the quickest practicable plan was to admit Superbike kit engines in artisan chassis (like those in Moto2), with subsidies from Dorna where appropriate. These so-called CRT machines were seconds a lap off the pace but did put teams and riders in place to gain experience for better equipment that was soon to come.

The extremity of this measure (which in fact went against MotoGP's original insistence on 'prototypes only') showed the manufacturers the extreme seriousness of the situation. Dorna had done what it could — it was time for the factories to step up. At the end of the 2013 season, the last for the CRTs, Honda showed its 'MotoGP production racer', the RCV1000R, beautifully finished but with its performance limited by steel valve springs (later a pneumatic-spring upgrade would take place). Now came the big breakthrough; the factories overcame their fears of technology leakage and agreed to provide year-old or two-year-old former team bikes to satellite teams under a scheme called the 'Open class' (in the past such bikes had often been crushed). Teams in 'Open' would use a

ABOVE The first step in Dorna's move to adopt first a common ECU and then common software came in 2014 with the use of this Magneti Marelli ECU on bikes in the 'Open' class.

to conserve their tyres so they would still have the grip to fight at the end, when the others were sliding. The greatest of these has been Marc Márquez, who developed his techniques through constant thoughtful improvisation. When, after two years in Moto2, Márquez advanced to MotoGP, he quickly found ways to achieve the necessary lap times, while using his tyre-conservation methods to defeat more experienced riders in the final laps. Moto2 has become the university of tyre management.

In 2012 Moto3 replaced 125 category with a single 250cc four-stroke cylinder of MotoGP dimensions,

RIGHT A Ducati electronics technician at work during the Valencia test at the close of the 2015 season.

common Marelli ECU with common software, and in return would be allowed 12 rather than six engines per rider, and 24 litres of fuel rather than 20. This result — reliable access to competitive equipment — was partly planned and partly the product of guiding the push-and-shove of racing politics.

Up to the time that World Superbike came under Dorna control (through Dorna's owner Bridgepoint acquiring Infront Sports), Honda — the elephant in the room — could threaten to move to that series if a rev limit or common software were imposed in MotoGP. When that door closed in 2012, the process of moving first to a common ECU (effective from 1 January 2014) and then to 2016's common software could begin.

Racing had for years been an all-out technology contest in which teams vied to develop engines and, later, software fastest. But because only the top teams had resources for this, grids had shrunk and Suzuki had dropped out. This made it clear that to survive and prosper, racing had to become a contest that all teams could afford — the exciting contest of machine set-up, tyre choice and rider wisdom that we see at every round through the four practices plus qualifying and

the race itself. That could not happen unless ECU and software became 'black boxes', identical for all entrants, and the engine 'arms race' was rationally controlled. Those tasks have now been accomplished.

When in 2012 Canada Pension Plan Investment Board took a 39 per cent stake in Dorna, its highly articulate spokeswoman told this writer, "We do extensive due diligence and have been impressed with Dorna's track record — the ability of the business to perform well through economic cycles. In the due diligence process we saw that motorcycle racing has global appeal with growth potential in emerging markets."

The 2016 season brought a result of the kind toward which Dorna has worked for years — nine different winning riders with participation from five manufacturer teams plus the satellite teams. As always in human affairs, good management is the thinking partner of happenstance. This was the year when all teams had to adapt to a new 'spec' tyre supplier, Michelin, and the factory teams were slowed by their struggle to achieve control through the common ECU and software.

Motorsport writers have now begun to observe that MotoGP is more spectacular than Formula One.

ABOVE Michelin returned to the MotoGP fray in 2016 as the sole tyre supplier.

CONTRIBUTORS

DENNIS NOYES
American journalist, author, broadcaster and former racer.

IGNACIO SAGNIER
Journalist and Communications Director of Dorna.

JUAN PEDRO DE LA TORRE
Spanish journalist and author involved in Grand Prix racing since 1988.

MICHAEL SCOTT
South African journalist, author and Editor of *Motocourse*.

MATTHEW MILES
American journalist and Digital Publishing Director at Bonnier Motorcycle Group.

STEFANO SARAGONI
Editor of *In Moto* (Italy) and former Editor of *Motosprint*.

JULIAN RYDER
British journalist, author and broadcaster.

MATT BIRT
British journalist and broadcaster, formerly Grand Prix reporter for *Motor Cycle News*.

NICK HARRIS
British author, journalist and broadcaster.

EMILIO PÉREZ DE ROZAS
Spanish journalist with *El Periódico de Catalunya*.

SATOSHI ENDO
Japanese Grand Prix journalist and photographer with *Tokyo Chunichi Sports*.

ENRICO BORGHI
Editor in Chief of *Motosprint* (Italy).

PAUL CARRUTHERS
Communications Manager at *MotoAmerica* and former Editor of *Cycle News*.

DON COX
Australian author and journalist.

GÜNTHER WIESINGER
Austrian who is Editor in Chief and Managing Director of *speedweek.com*.

THOMAS BAUJARD
MotoGP journalist for *Moto Journal* (France).

KEVIN CAMERON
American author and motorcycle journalist who is Technical Editor of *Cycle World*.

MARTIN RAINES
Compiler of Dorna's official MotoGP statistics.

ACKNOWLEDGEMENTS

FOR THEIR TESTIMONIES
Carmelo Ezpeleta
Enrique Aldama
Manel Arroyo
Jordi Pons
Pau Serracanta
Carles Jorba
Sergi Sendra
Pep Vila

FOR THEIR CONTINUOUS SUPPORT
Mark Hughes
Neil Spalding
Mat Oxley
Ernest Riveras
Peter Clifford
Judith Pieper-Köhler

FOR THEIR HELP AT DORNA
Michael Morel
Kim Navarro
Frances Wyld
Dylan Gray
Montse Sogues
Diego Sperani (photos)
Luca Gambuti (photos)
Oriol Morral (cover design)
Friné Velilla

PHOTOGRAPHERS
Marco Guidetti
Henk Keulemans
Werner Reiss
Alex Farinelli
Gold and Goose
Getty Images
Mortons Archive

PHOTOGRAPH CREDITS

2Snap 104 bottom, 114, 116 top, 118 bottom, 121 bottom, 122 top, 123, 127 top, 129, 131 bottom, 133 top, 139 top and bottom left, 142–143, 151, 160, 161, 172 bottom, 173 bottom, 180 top, 204 bottom, 205 top, 213 top.

Borghi, Enrico 190.

Dorna 5, 6, 7, 8–9, 11, 13, 17, 18 top, 21, 22-29, 30, 35, 36, 38, 39, 40, 41, 43, 44, 45, 49, 50 top, 52 top, 53, 54 bottom, 55, 58 top, 59 top, 62 top, 63, 69, 76, 77, 88, 93 top, 95 bottom, 97 bottom, 135, 136 top, 137 bottom, 138 top, 140, 141, 155, 167 bottom, 168, 169 top, 175, 176, 180 bottom, 181 top, 182, 183, 188 top, 189, 191 top, 192 top, 197 top, 200 top, 201 top, 208 bottom, 209 bottom, 215 top, 216 top, 218 top, 220, 221, 223

top, 228 bottom, 236 top, 239.

Getty Images 31 bottom, 46–47, 57, 60, 61 bottom, 156, 185 top, 192 bottom, 193 top, 211 top, 222.

Gold and Goose 4, 34, 130 top, 163, 202 top, 234, 235, 236 bottom, 237, 238.

Harris, Nick (collection of) 14 top, 15, 20 top.

Keulemans, Henk 12, 14 bottom, 20 bottom, 31 top, 32, 42, 50 bottom, 51, 64, 65 top, 66, 67, 68, 69 bottom, 70, 71 top, 72, 73, 74 top, 75, 79, 80, 81 bottom, 82, 83, 84 top, 85, 86, 87 top, 89, 90, 91, 92 top, 93 bottom, 95 top, 96, 97 top, 98, 99, 100 bottom, 101, 102 top and bottom left, 103 top, 104 top, 105,

106 top, 107, 108, 109, 110 top and bottom right, 111 top, 112, 113, 115 top, 116 bottom, 117 bottom, 118 top, 119, 120 top, 121 top, 122 bottom, 124, 125 top, 126, 128, 131 top, 132, 133 bottom, 134 top, 137 top, 138 bottom, 139 bottom right, 145, 148, 149, 150, 152, 153, 154, 158, 159, 162, 170, 172 top, 173 top, 177 bottom, 178, 179, 185 bottom, 186 top, 187, 194, 195 top, 196, 197 bottom, 198, 199, 201 bottom, 202 bottom, 203, 206, 208 top, 210, 211 bottom, 212 top, 213 bottom, 215 bottom, 218 bottom, 219, 224 bottom, 225, 226, 227, 228 top, 229, 232, 233.

Mortons Archive 54 top, 56, 157, 167 top, 169 bottom, 184 top, 207.

Noyes, Dennis (collection of) 10.

Raines, Martin (collection of) 16, 18 bottom, 19, 37, 48, 52 bottom, 58 bottom, 59 bottom, 61 top, 62 bottom, 65 bottom, 71 bottom, 74 bottom, 78, 81 top, 84 bottom, 87 bottom, 92 bottom, 94 bottom, 100 top, 102 bottom right, 103 bottom, 106 bottom, 110 bottom left, 111 bottom, 115 bottom, 117 top, 120 bottom, 125 bottom, 127 bottom, 130 bottom, 134 bottom, 136 bottom, 166 bottom, 171 bottom, 174 bottom, 177 bottom, 181 bottom, 184 bottom, 186 bottom, 188 bottom, 191 bottom, 193 bottom, 195 bottom, 200 bottom, 204 top, 205 bottom, 209 top, 212 bottom, 214 bottom, 216 bottom, 223 bottom, 224 top.

Reiss, Werner 217.